As one of Beck Center's most generous supporters, it is a pleasure to give you this history book, *Celebrating Our Past – Creating Our Future*. Philanthropic leaders like you are the reason our community has enjoyed 90 years of arts experiences from this organization. Here's to many more years to come!

Best wishes for a happy and healthy 2023!

Cindy Einhouse

"The life of the arts, far from being an interruption, a distraction, in the life of a nation, is close to the center of a nation's purpose -- and is a test of the quality of a nation's civilization."

-- John F. Kennedy

Knowing that you are as conscious of the stewardship of our operating dollars as we are, please be assured that it cost Beck Center less than $10 to purchase and mail each author copy of this book.

TABLE OF CONTENTS

FORWARD AND DEDICATION:

"Celebrating Our Past; Creating Our Future" is dedicated to the thousands of artists, performers, volunteers, faculty, staff, and donors who gave their hearts and souls to build this organization which has brought great joy and artistry to so many. It would be impossible to list them all, as it would be impossible to list all of the many individuals, foundations, corporations, government entities, and organizations which have provided philanthropic support over the years, but each was critical to the growth and development of what is now one of the largest arts education and performance institutions in Ohio.

The history of this organization is so vast and complex, no doubt there are important parts which have inadvertently been left out. Indeed, between the time that the writing has been completed on this book and it is on sale to the public, there might be enough notes taken on what is missing that another book could be written.

Any and all proceeds from the sale of this book will be used to create and sustain an endowment for future generations to enjoy arts experiences at Beck Center for the Arts. BeckCenter.org/give

"Beck Center was my second home. I can't tell you how many times I would get to the theater even an hour early, just so I could be there, because I felt so safe, happy and loved in that building. Being surrounded by art in every form was such an invaluable experience as a child." Rory O'Malley

1997 - Youth Theater production, *Narnia,* directed by Ellen Huber
Photo credit Beck Center
Tony Award Nominee Rory O'Malley (left) as Mr. Tumnus
Senior Editor for Marvel Comics Nicholas Lowe (right) as Aslan

CHAPTER 1:

Beck Center for the Arts on its 90th Anniversary – 1933-2023

Come along on a journey through time, where the love of humanity-affirming experiences brought people together and kept them together for over nine decades, through the Great Depression, World War II, and a Global Pandemic. What began as an all-volunteer community theater known as The Lakewood Little Theatre in 1933 has evolved into a vibrant community arts center, serving more than 60,000 people each year throughout five counties of Northeast Ohio.

2011 - *Hairspray* - photo credit Kathy Sandham

Beck Center for the Arts is the only non-profit organization in Northeast Ohio dedicated to creating an individual arts experience for all people by delivering a personal, intimate professional theater experience and comprehensive, curriculum-based education with a focus on community outreach and partnerships in order to enrich the Northeast Ohio community.

We create art experiences.

At Beck Center for the Arts, we strive to create an arts experience that is as individual as the people it serves. Our theater experience is personal and intimate – close enough to interact with the performance and feel part of it. As the leader in comprehensive arts education in Northeast Ohio, we offer wide-ranging, curriculum-based arts education founded on the desire to engage children in the arts and, ultimately, in lifelong learning. Overall, we are committed to creating an individual arts experience for people at all ability and experience levels because we believe that this can be transformative and strengthening for them and their communities.

Engaged and personal professional theater experience
Sometimes when you go to professional theater productions, you are entertained but may feel as if you are watching from afar. At Beck Center for the Arts, immersion is important. Whether we are presenting a musical, comedy or drama, we are committed to providing you with the highest quality theater production. A theater experience with diverse and eclectic programming where you are close enough to become involved in the performance, interact with it and feel part of it. At Beck Center for the Arts, we offer an intimate theater experience with the kind of personal engagement that larger theaters simply can't provide.

The leader in comprehensive arts education in Northeast Ohio
Beck Center for the Arts offers curriculum-based arts education in dance, music, theater, visual arts and Creative Arts Therapies for all ability levels and ages, including early childhood. With over 300 arts education classes each week, we give individualized attention to all participants. At the core of our arts education program is our desire to introduce children to the arts, move them on to higher levels of the arts, and ultimately motivate them to embrace the lifelong learning process.

A focus on bringing an arts experience to the community through partnerships and outreach
At Beck Center for the Arts, we believe in bringing an arts experience to the Northeast Ohio community in a number of ways, through participation in festivals and community events, and a wide variety of activities such as assemblies, field trips, workshops, teacher in-services and on-site performances for schools and other community organizations. Our visual arts exhibitions are always free and open to the public, twelve months every year. We are a leader in collaborating with diverse community groups and venues such as The Rock and Roll Hall of Fame and Museum, Cleveland Botanical Garden, and Baldwin Wallace University, to name a few, and have partnered in many special events. We are dedicated to enriching our community through the arts.

Photo credit Wetzler Studios

Creating an individual arts experience for all people

Beck Center for the Arts has an eclectic selection of performances to suit many tastes and a wide range of classes, lessons and programs to accommodate all ability levels. This diverse arts experience not only encourages our students to stretch their artistic potential but also develops

a heightened awareness and emotional and cognitive engagement for all who participate. We believe that arts experiences can be transformative and strengthens the cultural development of our community.

A beacon for relevant and meaningful programming, Beck Center has become one of the largest producers of musical theater in Northeast Ohio and one of the top five performing arts centers in the greater Cleveland area. Over 26,000 individuals attended Beck Center theater performances in 2018-19, which is the

Photo credit Kim Parrish

organization's greatest attendance recorded prior to the 2020 Global Pandemic.

In 2021, each week, over 3,000 individuals are served through Arts Education programs. Over 780 classes, lessons, and programs are offered in dance, music, theater, visual arts, as well as in outreach education and creative arts therapies. Typically, approximately 4,200 adults and children are reached each year through customized field trips, workshops, residencies and matinees. The Creative Arts Therapies program provides music therapy, art therapy, adapted dance, adapted theater and inclusive arts experiences that welcome individuals, regardless of ability. This includes sensory friendly programming, providing individuals with disabilities and sensory challenges a welcoming and accepting environment.

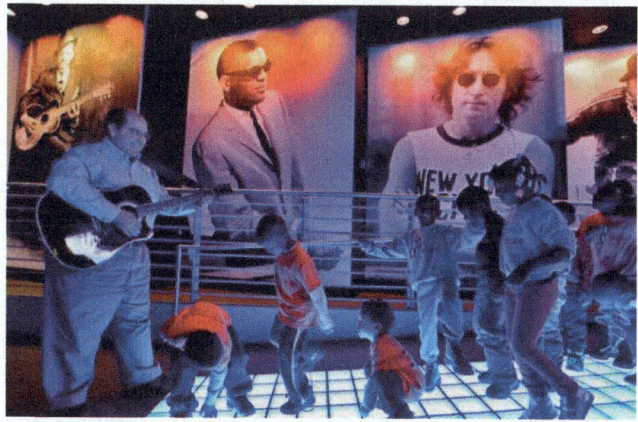

Early Childhood classes are offered for children and their caregivers from birth to six years as introduction to the arts in developmentally appropriate contexts. Classes encourage play, creativity, cooperation, attention, and provide caregivers with activities to continue at home. Adults are offered a range of classes including private and group sessions for those who wish to hone their skills or make new connections and work with like-minded artists. Beck Center's faculty and staff are committed to providing

Ed Gallagher at the Rock & Roll Hall of Fame – "Toddler Rock"

accessible arts experiences to everyone, regardless of age or ability.

As of 2022, Beck Center's mission was "to inspire, enrich, and transform lives through dynamic arts experiences." Its vision was "connecting and empowering people, communities, and cultures to flourish through excellent arts experiences." Beck Center values were stated as follows:

We believe in:
- Sharing the transforming and transcending power of the arts
- Pursuing excellence as vital to our programming and operations
- Cultivating an inclusive, accessible, and safe environment
- Nurturing relationships through compassion, service, and personal attention
- Exemplifying diversity, equity, and inclusion in all we do
- Collaborating and building relationships
- Manifesting accountable stewardship for the organization and its resources

All of this was not created overnight, but rather developed and evolved over the past 90 years because of the devotion of countless individuals. And it all started with the Little Theatre movement.

Musical Theater students; photo credit Wetzler Studios

"All of the Little Theatres are in one way or another the expression of a revolt against the flashy plays of Broadway...Little Theatre workers want to better the community, further the art, keep alive the best drama already produced elsewhere – an opportunity to act, paint, design." Charles Parkhurst, 1929

CHAPTER 2:
The Inspiration of the Little Theatre Movement – 1910-1930

As the new medium of cinema began to compete with live theater, the Little Theatre Movement developed in the United States, from about 1912 to 1925. Little Theatres provided experimental centers for amateurs in the dramatic arts. In large cities such as Chicago, Boston, Seattle, and Detroit, companies formed to produce more intimate, non-commercial, non-profit, and reform-minded entertainment.

The American Little Theatre Movement of the early 20th century was the result of young actors, directors, designers, and others who were influenced and inspired by European theatre, particularly in Paris, Berlin, and Moscow. The European Independent Theatre Movement was a rebellion against commercial or professional theaters and was characterized by simple scenery, original repertory, and experimentation.

At the peak of the movement, dozens of Little Theatre groups across the country presented vibrant, local alternatives to mainstream commercial theater. Little Theatres started as community theaters and university drama programs. Numerous small companies flourished, creating environments for diverse voices and viewpoints.

In 1929, Charles Chandler Parkhurst traced the Little Theatre movement from its origin in Europe to its growth in the United States in his Boston University Master of Arts thesis. He wrote "the Little Theatre grew out of a natural wish to have good plays presented for 'Art's Sake,' free from any commercial aspects." Billboard and Variety magazines devoted pages to amateur theater. Metropolitan newspapers gave frequent notices of amateur productions and ran columns about the Little Theatre. Publishers flooded the market with plays intended for amateurs and books were published about Little Theatre organization, management, and production techniques. Almost every college and university established a dramatic arts department or theater school and hundreds of public schools sponsored dramatic societies.

Manhattan's Washington Square Players was founded as a Little Theatre in 1914. The Provincetown Players, which started as a Little Theatre in 1915, produced Eugene O'Neill's first one-act plays. In 1915, Cleveland Play House began as a Little Theatre.

About Cleveland Play House, Mr. Parkhurst wrote "Here we find a director and a group of men and women interested in the theatre as a fine art and able to practice this fine art with sufficient skill to attract as audience those other people in the city who desire to see it so practiced and have too scant an opportunity in the professional playhouses." He noted that the American Little Theatre was the driving force of creative people who wanted to express themselves but were unwilling or unable to find an opening in professional theater.

The Little Theatre became a home for talented individuals looking for an outlet for self-expression, creative enjoyment, and a like-minded community. Mr. Parkhurst believed that "all of the Little Theatres are in one way or another the expression of a revolt against the flashy plays of Broadway." He wrote "Little Theatre workers want to better the community, to further the art, to keep alive the best drama already produced elsewhere, an opportunity to act, paint, design."

Little Theatres challenged commercial theater models by creating small theaters that could be more artistically daring, according to Baylor University Theatre History professor Dr. Deanna Toten Beard. She notes that the movement sought to improve economic conditions in American theater, foster greater artistic exploration, and promote new plays by American playwrights.

"The movie theater is never going away. If that was a case why are there still restaurants? People still have kitchens in their home!" (Michael Moore)

CHAPTER 3:

In The Meantime...

Given that the origin of the Little Theatre Movement was a revolt against the commercialization of theater and cinema, it is ironic that The Lakewood Little Theatre would ultimately land in a movie theater. In the dawn of the 20th century, movie theaters were springing up all around the country. According to the Lakewood Historical Society website, "Entertainment in Lakewood: Movie Theaters," by 1924, at a time when the population was 40,000, Lakewood had at least seven theaters. One of these seven Lakewood theaters was the 500-seat Lucier Theatre at 17823 Detroit Avenue.

The property was purchased by Lambert Lucier from Solon Colohan in 1914 (consisting of 59ft on Detroit Avenue, 179ft on the east side, 57ft on the south side and 162ft on the west side). Mr. Lucier was a barber in the 1900 Census, born in Canada, and an insurance solicitor in the 1910 Census, single in both. In 1914 he was living at 1536 Wayne Avenue. He died in 1918, and his estate sold the property to Blanche Maheu in 1920, according to research conducted in October, 2021 by Katharine Ott (Lakewood Historical Society volunteer).

Blanche Kolar Maheu was married to Albert "Bert" C. Maheu[1] who was hired by Lambert Lucier to build the Lucier Theatre. Some sources indicate that the theatre was built in 1915, however,

there are movie advertisements dated December 1914. Bert Maheu later owned and operated the Lucier Theatre along with a candy store next door, at the corner of Wayne and Detroit Avenues from about 1926 until 1930 when the family lost the property in the Depression.

Albert "Bert" Maheu – photo credit Maheu family

---

[1] Albert Charles "Bert" Maheu (1883-1961) built and owned the Lucier Theatre, storefronts and apartments. In 1912, he was listed as an architect with an office in downtown Cleveland's Arcade. Bert and his wife Margaret Elizabeth "Blanche" also owned a tavern and a candy/soda fountain. They had three children – William Albert (1905-1937), Mabel Blanche (1907-1996), and Bertram Clarence "Bert" (1913-2001). Three of Bertram Clarence "Bert"'s seven children – Bertram Charles "Bud," Carole, and Maggie – contributed to this book. Bert was active in the Lakewood Follies, a group of golden-agers who performed in nursing homes and hospitals. The family flew in to Lakewood, Ohio in the early 1990s to see the Lakewood Follies perform at Beck Center/Lakewood Little Theatre.

LUCIER
Lakewood's Most Exclusive Photoplay
Theater, Showing

ZUDORA
DECEMBER 14TH.

Photos copied with permission from the Maheu family – Carole Maheu Ritter
Maheu Candy Store on the corner of Wayne and Detroit Avenues, 1914, (L-R, Mabel Maheu, Willie Maheu, Albert Maheu)

We hereby certify that we have examined the premises described on the reverse side hereof, an accurate plat of which is shown below, and find that there is located entirely thereon a 2 story, brick and stucco, tar and gravel roof building, now known as Nos.17811-17813-17815-17817-17821-17823-17825 Detroit Street,(Detroit Avenue according to Street sign). We also find that there is located entirely thereon a 1-1/2 story,frame,tar paper roof building. Said premises bear no house number. A photograph of said premises was taken on June 28,1926,and is printed hereon. We find the buildings upon said premises to be entirely within the lot lines and that there are no encroachments of any character of adjoining properties. Said plat shows the dimensions of the lot and the location and dimensions of the buildings together with any rights of easement. Said premises are now occupied by The Great Atlantic and Pacific Tea Company,and others,which claim to be the tenants of Blanche E. Maheu.

This certificate is made for and at the instance of The Mutual Benefit Life Association.

Cleveland, Ohio, June 28, 1926.

The Guarantee Title and Trust Company,

By

Thos. C. Terrett

Vice Pres't
& Ass't Sec'y

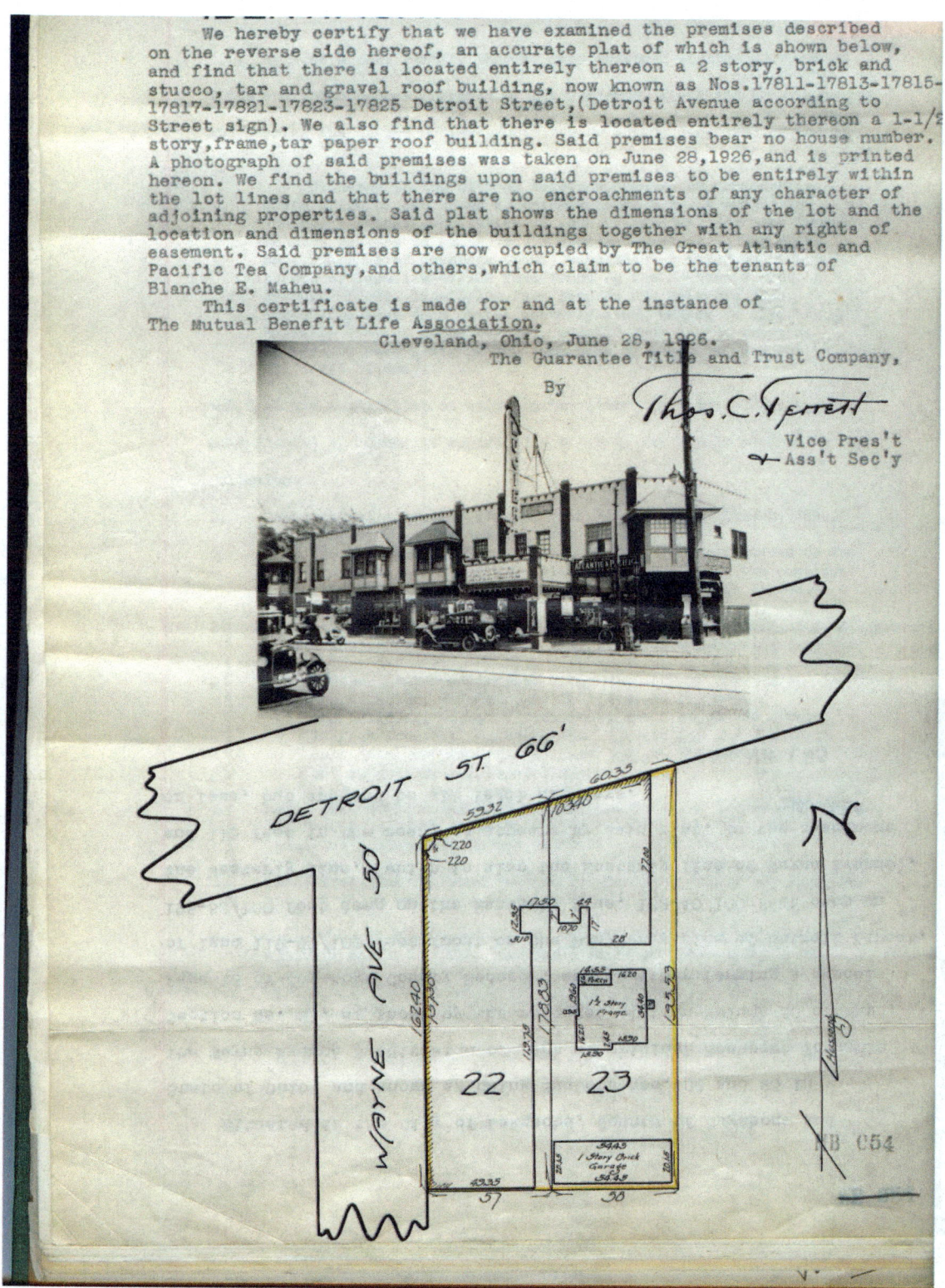

June 28, 1926 - Photo credit The Guarantee Title and Trust Company

1927 – photo credit Maheu family

New Lucier Opens With Sound Device Installed

Equipment for reproducing talkies and sound pictures has been installed in the New Lucier, 17823 Detroit Avenue, Lakewood, which opens today under new management with Patsy Ruth Miller featured in "The Fall of Eve."

The theater has been completely redecorated, equipped with new projection machines and numerous other facilities, Bert C. Maheu, the manager, announced.

The Patsy Ruth Miller film will continue its run until Wednesday, when Neil Hamilton's "Studio Murder Mystery" opens, a two-day run. Eddie Dowling will be presented in "The Rainbow Man" on Friday and Saturday.

Moran 'n Mack Back

"The Two Black Crows," Moran and Mack, are back on the vaudeville stage after a short respite during which they made some talkies.

Tug o' War on Organ.

Frank Gallagher, organist at M. B.

"Wheezer," "Farina" and "Tige" are back at the State this week in a new Our Gang comedy. Farina, the little sepia actress, comes through with one good gag after another in this all-talking picture.

Spooky costumes worn by her playmates of the gang give Farina the blues."

Unknown date – Maheu Candy Store and soda fountain at 17825 Detroit Avenue; (L-R) Albert's sons Willie and Bert

Models made by William Maheu in 1929

Models made by William (Willie) Maheu in 1929; Photo provided by Maggie Maheu Milburn

The earliest advertisement for the Lucier Theatre available through research was on December 6, 1914[2] and the latest ad (a one-line listing) was on December 14, 1937, when the Lucier showed "Broadway Melody of 1938" starring Robert Taylor and Eleanor Powell, and "Rootin' Tootin' Rhythm" starring Gene Autry. It appears the Lucier was in business as a movie theater for 23 years.

---

[2] Although a Plain Dealer article about the Lucier Theatre was dated 1914, the Cuyahoga County Auditor's site indicates that "part 1" of the building was built in 1915 and "part 2" was built in 1925. No further explanation was included.

In a Plain Dealer news article dated December 27, 1914, the Lucier Theatre was described as Lakewood's most beautiful theater, and that the management had specialized in securing the very best in dramatic and comedy features, for its demanding and exclusive patrons.

An advertisement in the Plain Dealer on September 29, 1929, announced that a "new" Lucier opened under new management, completely redecorated, with new projection machines and "equipment for reproducing talkies and sound pictures" installed. Bert C. Maheu was listed as the manager.

An article in the Plain Dealer on November 23, 1930, announced the Lucier's reopening "after a week's darkness with a new manager and new sound equipment." Four Marx Brothers' movies including "Animal Crackers" were selected by the new manager J.E. Surrell.

On August 6, 1933, the Plain Dealer announced a Double Feature Bill in the newly re-opened Lucier Theater, under new management – J.O. Guthrie and F. G. Schram – as well as the installation of new sound equipment. On December 17, 1933, a line appeared in the Plain Dealer announcing that the Lucier was closed for the installation of a new heating system and would re-open "within a week or so."

The family of Mr. Maheu states that the property was lost during the Depression, which would account for the announcement of new management in 1930. Mr. Maheu apparently maintained an interest in the area since he purchased a tavern across the street (17900 Detroit Avenue) at the end of 1933 or early 1934, and operated it through 1958 as B. Maheu's Tavern. The "Cavern" was a ratskeller (an additional basement bar) during that time.

November 1939 - B. Maheu's Tavern (Albert "Bert" Maheu), 17900 Detroit Avenue, Lakewood Ohio, across the street from the Lucier. The building was built in 1920, and operated as a grocery store (1920-25), barbershop (1926-31), and gym for boxers (1932-1933), prior to becoming Maheu's Tavern. (Research by Ross Bassett)
Photo credit unknown – Beck Center Archives

Maheu's New Year's Eve Party ticket (The Cavern was in the basement of the Tavern)

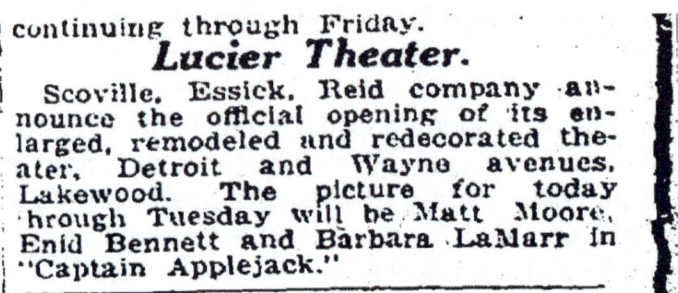

In spring of 2016, Greg Palumbo, then executive director of the Lakewood Historical Society, wrote an article for their newsletter about Lakewood theaters and included several photos associated with the Lucier (pictured below).

Children's Bargain Matinee coupon from either 1919 or 1930, based on the ticket dates - From the Lakewood Historical Society Archives

A 1916 program from the Lucier Theatre – Lakewood Historical Society Archives

"The idea of a Little Theatre for Lakewood if not born within the (Lakewood) Junior Chamber (of Commerce) has nevertheless had its inspiration rekindled there, and but for the untiring aid of the Chamber and its encouragement and support, its promotion as an actuality might never have been attempted by the Guild. The Chamber ever working for the progress and betterment of Lakewood, has again proven itself worthy of the title as one of the foremost civic organizations in this city." (from the Guild of the Masques Playbill, 1932)

CHAPTER 4:

Where It All Began – 1930-1933

In April 1930, the Lakewood Junior Chamber of Commerce voted as one of their major projects to sponsor a Little Theatre group in Lakewood, Ohio, providing a higher type of dramatic art which was considered by many to have fallen into sad neglect during this era of cinema productions. At that time, there were twelve such small theater groups in Lakewood which, no doubt like others around the country, were made up of creative people who wanted to express themselves through the arts. London-trained director Richard Kay[3] was commissioned to attempt to incorporate the Little Theatre groups into one good strong organization.

The different groups which were contacted were willing to have one group, but each wanted to be the leading organization and have the others join their group. So, Richard Kay formed a completely new group called the Guild of the Masques on February 9, 1931, with founding members Richard and Catherine (sometimes spelled Kathryn) Kay, Clarice and Robert Seibert, Doris and Edwin Killer, Lloyd and Ruth Taylor, Evelyn and Arthur Grove, Charles and Hilda Robinson, Ronald and Winifred Skyrme, Everett McCurdy, Mary Ann Lind, and Ray Enright. The purpose of the Guild was to promote interest in the study of Dramatic Art in all its phases, to produce plays for public and private showing, and to participate in Little Theatre activities.

---

[3] From Paul Kiser regarding his wife Sara 'Saralinda' Seibert Kiser's family history: Saralinda's father is Dr. David Seibert. David's mother was Clarice Kay Seibert and her brother/his uncle, Richard Kay, was the founder of the Lakewood Little Theater. According to his U.S. citizenship application, Richard came to the United States on 12 May 1922. This move put the family in Cleveland/Lakewood, Ohio area where Richard established himself as an accountant. There is no family narrative of why they all went directly from northern England to Cleveland, but it is possible that Ruth's (the oldest sister) husband had a connection to the area. Richard married Catherine Helm in 1930. His 1937 U.S. citizenship application incorrectly states the marriage to Catherine as 1920; however, the marriage license was issued in 1930. Richard, Catherine, and the Seibert families moved to California in the early 1950s and he lived there until his death in 1960.

Mary Bagshaw Kay, the mother, died in Cleveland in 1945. The oldest sister, Ruth Kay Wallis, later spelled Wallace, likely lived out the rest of her life in the Cleveland area. His brother, John Bagshaw Kay also likely lived out his life there. Clarice's twin sister, Doris Kay Killer or Killear was still living in Lakewood as of the 1940 census.

Richard Kay

The Guild grew to twenty members who met and rehearsed in their Lakewood living rooms and presented three productions annually on school stages. They performed their first play, "The Queen's Husband" on June 17 and 18, 1931 in a Sunday-school room of the West Side Evangelical Church at 38th and Bridge, Cleveland Ohio. (Robert Sherwood, the playwright of "The Queen's Husband," went on to win four Pulitzer Prizes just a few years later.) Members of the Junior Chamber were invited to the performance, and they were so impressed that they made it possible for the group to use the auditorium of Lakewood High School. In November of 1931, they sponsored the same play at Lakewood High School, charging 40 cents per ticket, to which nearly 1700 people attended.

1931 – photo credit Kay family

According to family member Becky Seibert, the soldier with the tall hat is Robert Seibert. The bride is Richard Kay's wife Catherine Helm Kay. The twins are Richard Kay's sisters Clarice Kay Seibert and Doris Kay Killear. (The family later changed the spelling to Killear from Killer as written in the playbill)

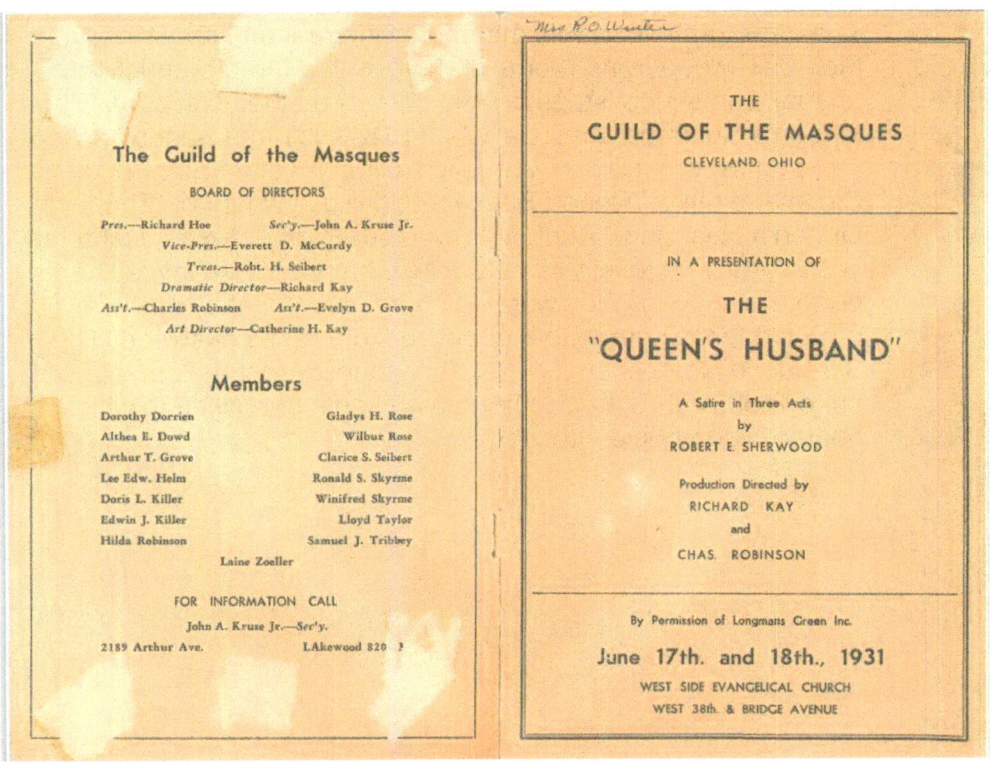

First playbill cover – *The Queen's Husband* – June 17 and 18, 1931

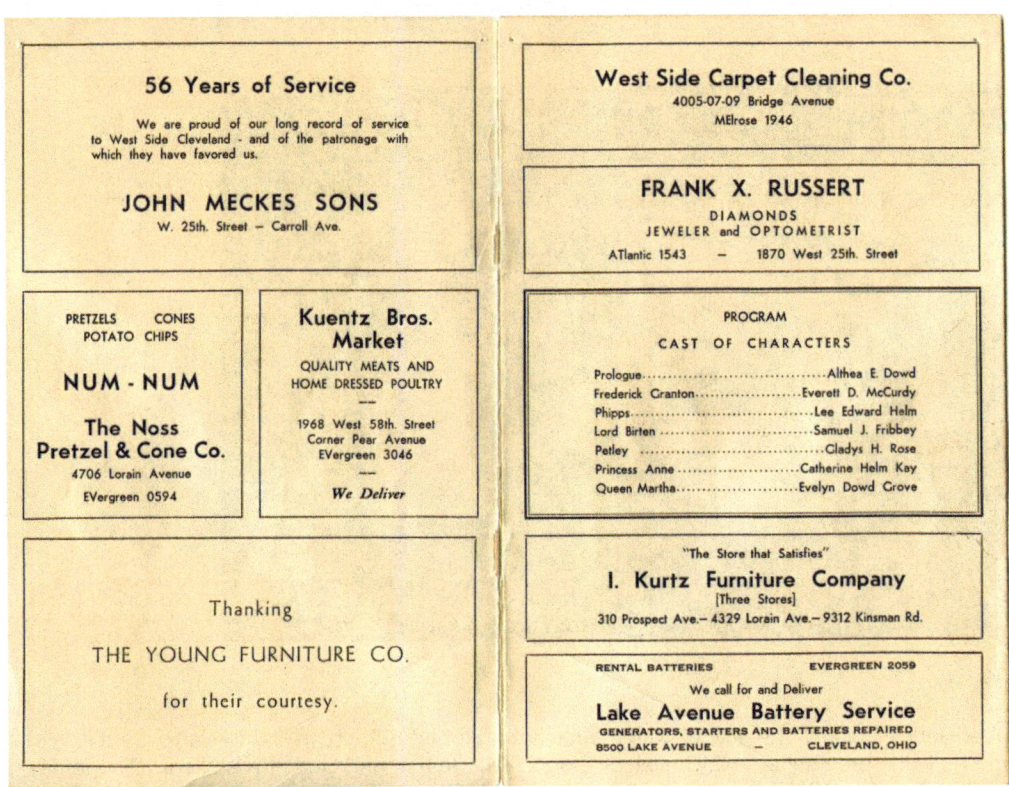

The Queen's Husband, playbill pages 2-3

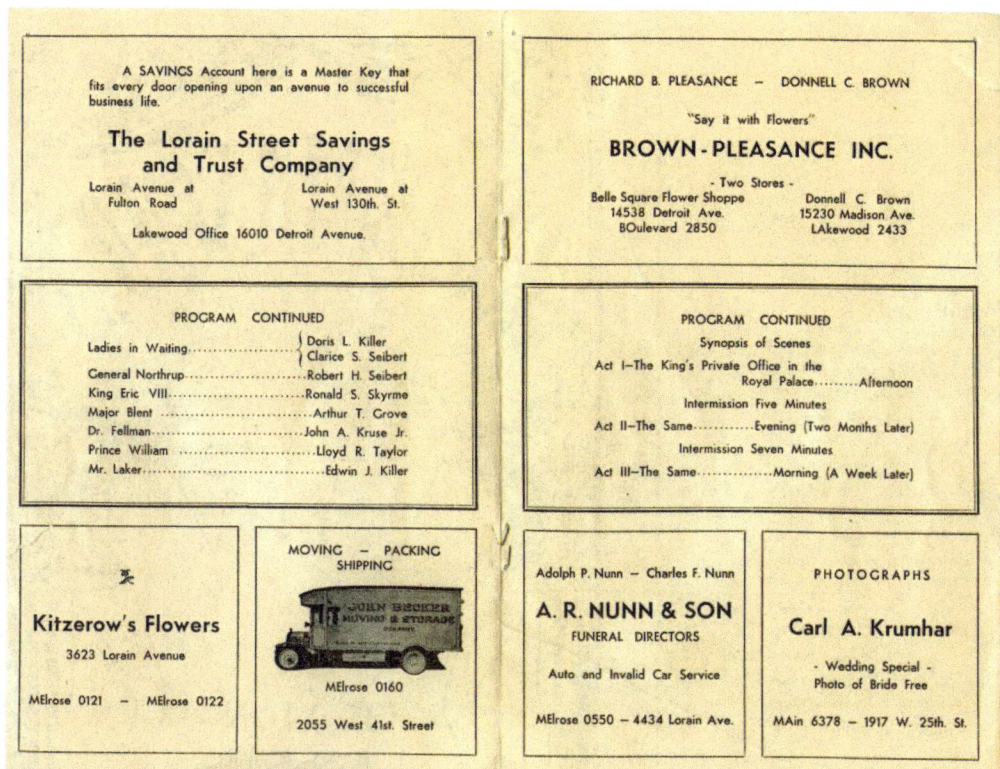

PROGRAM CONTINUED

Ladies in Waiting	Doris L. Killer
	Clarice S. Seibert
General Northrup	Robert H. Seibert
King Eric VIII	Ronald S. Skyrme
Major Blent	Arthur T. Grove
Dr. Fellman	John A. Kruse Jr.
Prince William	Lloyd R. Taylor
Mr. Laker	Edwin J. Killer

PROGRAM CONTINUED

Synopsis of Scenes

Act I—The King's Private Office in the
Royal Palace............Afternoon

Intermission Five Minutes

Act II—The Same............Evening (Two Months Later)

Intermission Seven Minutes

Act III—The Same............Morning (A Week Later)

The Queen's Husband, playbill pages 4-5

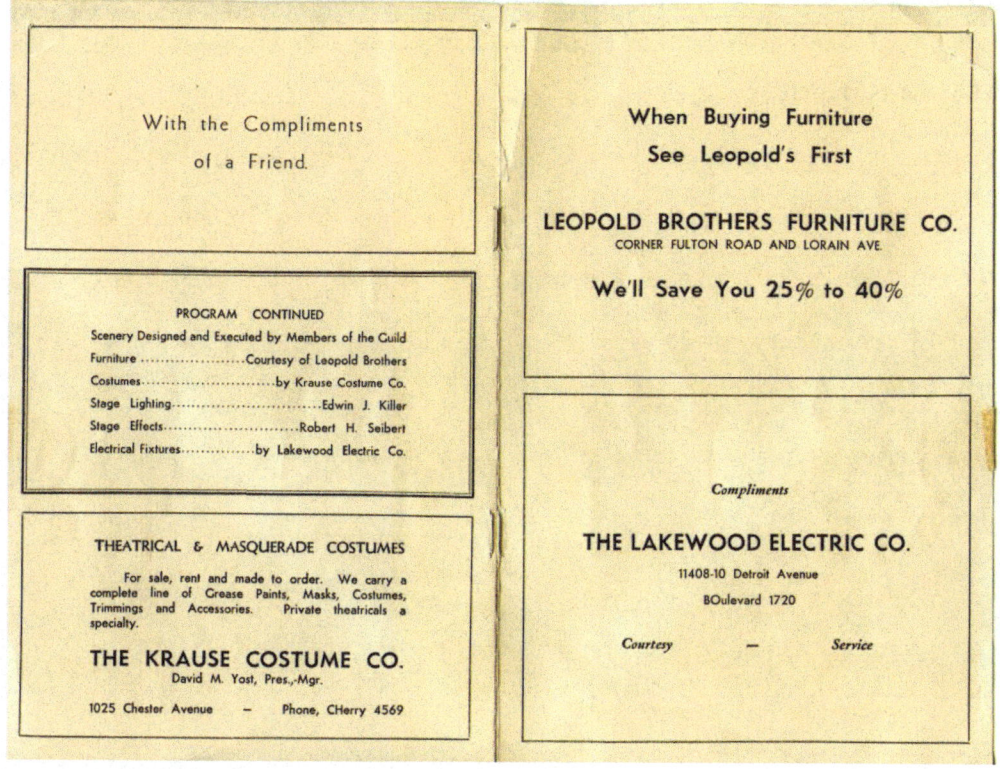

PROGRAM CONTINUED

Scenery Designed and Executed by Members of the Guild	
Furniture	Courtesy of Leopold Brothers
Costumes	by Krause Costume Co.
Stage Lighting	Edwin J. Killer
Stage Effects	Robert H. Seibert
Electrical Fixtures	by Lakewood Electric Co.

The Queen's Husband, playbill pages 6-7

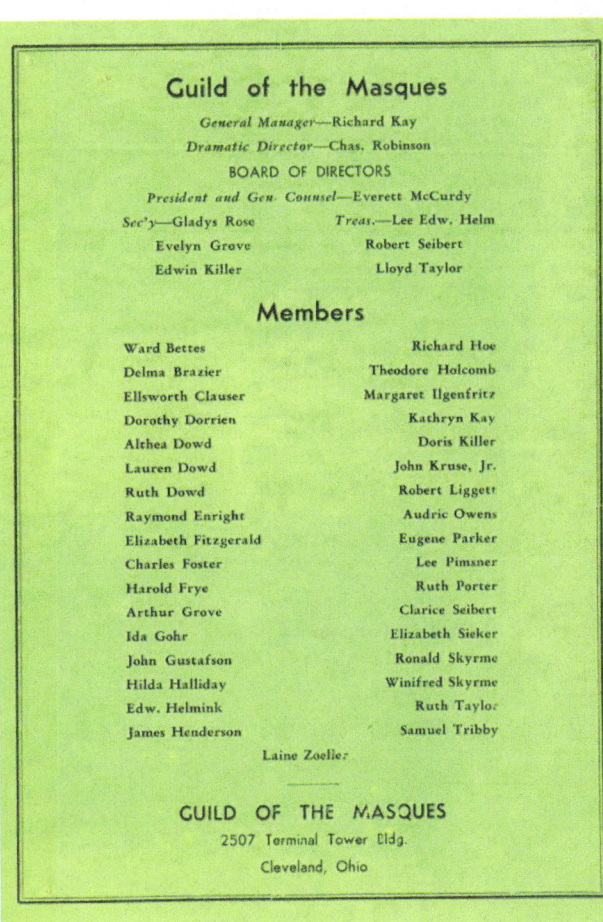

Guild of the Masques

General Manager—Richard Kay
Dramatic Director—Chas. Robinson
BOARD OF DIRECTORS
President and Gen. Counsel—Everett McCurdy
Sec'y—Gladys Rose   *Treas.*—Lee Edw. Helm
Evelyn Grove   Robert Seibert
Edwin Killer   Lloyd Taylor

Members

Ward Bettes	Richard Hoe
Delma Brazier	Theodore Holcomb
Ellsworth Clauser	Margaret Ilgenfritz
Dorothy Dorrien	Kathryn Kay
Althea Dowd	Doris Killer
Lauren Dowd	John Kruse, Jr.
Ruth Dowd	Robert Liggett
Raymond Enright	Audric Owens
Elizabeth Fitzgerald	Eugene Parker
Charles Foster	Lee Pimsner
Harold Frye	Ruth Porter
Arthur Grove	Clarice Seibert
Ida Gohr	Elizabeth Sieker
John Gustafson	Ronald Skyrme
Hilda Halliday	Winifred Skyrme
Edw. Helmink	Ruth Taylor
James Henderson	Samuel Tribby

Laine Zoeller

GUILD OF THE MASQUES

2507 Terminal Tower Bldg.
Cleveland, Ohio

Guild of the Masques First Season 1931-1932

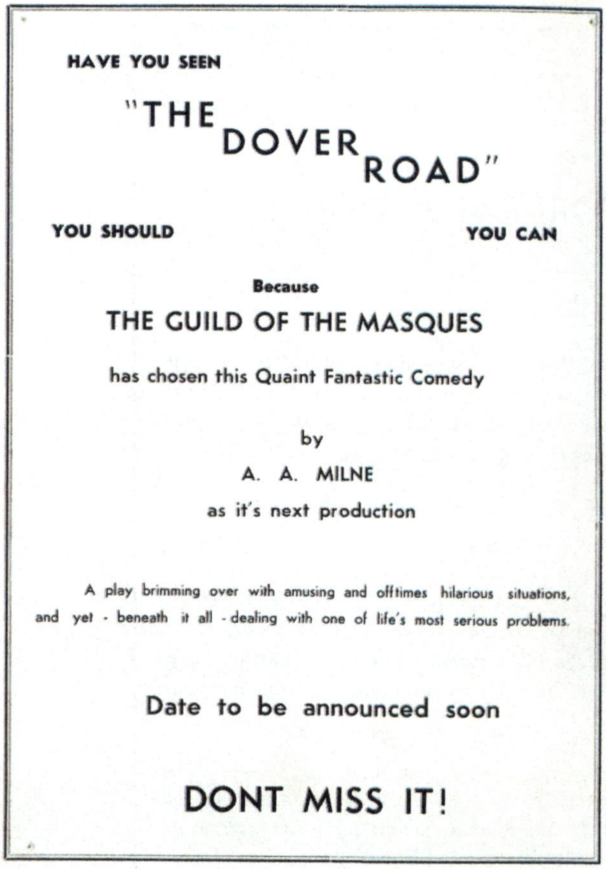

HAVE YOU SEEN

"THE DOVER ROAD"

YOU SHOULD   YOU CAN

Because

THE GUILD OF THE MASQUES

has chosen this Quaint Fantastic Comedy

by

A. A. MILNE

as it's next production

A play brimming over with amusing and offtimes hilarious situations,
and yet - beneath it all - dealing with one of life's most serious problems.

Date to be announced soon

DONT MISS IT!

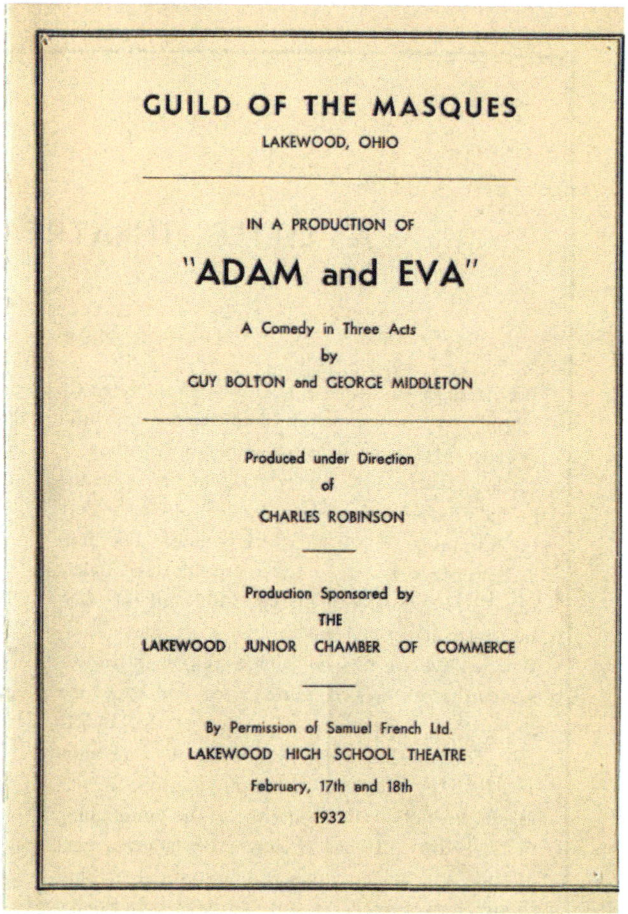

GUILD OF THE MASQUES

LAKEWOOD, OHIO

IN A PRODUCTION OF

"ADAM and EVA"

A Comedy in Three Acts
by
GUY BOLTON and GEORGE MIDDLETON

Produced under Direction
of
CHARLES ROBINSON

Production Sponsored by
THE
LAKEWOOD JUNIOR CHAMBER OF COMMERCE

By Permission of Samuel French Ltd.
LAKEWOOD HIGH SCHOOL THEATRE

February, 17th and 18th

1932

1932 Playbill – The Guild of the Masques at Lakewood High School Theatre

A LITTLE THEATRE FOR LAKEWOOD

WITH the inspiration of a Little Theatre already established and prospering in Cleveland the Guild of the Masques is courageously advocating a Little Theatre for Lakewood, not as a vague probability for the distant future, but a project the beginning at least of which is here. The final accomplishment, of course, depends on Lakewood's reception both of the Guild and the idea, but may be hoped for in the next few years. Whether we are to have such a cultural advancement of which there is a great need, and by which so many in Lakewood hope to offset that of the East Side of Cleveland, depends upon each individual. The Guild of the Masques feels it has talent worthy of the support of the community in this effort. It has already given a great deal of time and labor to this end, and stands willing to give its entire energy if it can have Lakewood's support.

Any mention of such a movement, or of the Guild of the Masques, cannot be made without recognition of the Lakewood Junior Chamber of Commerce. It has backed the production of "The Queen's Husband" and "Adam and Eva" with its entire organization. The idea of a Little Theatre for Lakewood if not born within the Junior Chamber has nevertheless had its inspiration rekindled there, and but for the untiring aid of the Chamber and its encouragement and support, its promotion as an actuality might never have been attempted by the Guild. The Chamber ever working for the progress and betterment of Lakewood, has again proven itself worthy of the title as one of the foremost civic organizations in this city.

The Board of Education, by placing at the disposal of the Guild, the High School Theatre, deserves high commendation from the community and has the warmest appreciation of the Guild.

You can aid in the advancement of this movement in many ways by your favorable comment to your friends, if you feel we deserve it, your criticism if you think we do not; by indorsing its support by your clubs, and organizations of which you are a member and most of all by your presence at performances and by bringing your friends.

Future productions are now under way. The next, to be produced shortly, is "The Dover Road." Here is a quaint, fantastic comedy, a mixture of Barrie and Stevenson.

This is a play; brimming over with amusing and oftimes hilarious situations, yet beneath it all -- dealing with one of lifes most serious problems. Ann and Leonard are taking the "Dover Road" -- and so are Eustasia and Nicholas -- but Mr. Latimer extends his hospitality so "irresistably" -- and points out a few little facts regarding the future which his "guests" have apparently overlooked.

This is one of A. A. Milne's most delightful plays and is now being rehearsed by the Guild, to be presented in the very near future.

Some of Mr. Milne's well known plays are "Mr Pim Passes By," "The Ivory Door," "The Truth about Blayds," "Ariadne," etc.

If you desire to be placed on our mailing list we shall notify you of future performances.

From the Guild of the Masques Playbill 1932

A series of plays were then given at the high school, under the general supervision of the Lakewood Department of Recreation, but the school was growing. When it became impossible for the Guild to continue there, they moved on to Hayes School.

The Guild sought a location with better proximity to public transportation, and the group settled on Gormsan's Hall at 18517 Detroit Avenue (what became Bonne Bell headquarters and later Onix). The third floor lodge room, a meeting room of the Knights of Pythius, was rented and a portable stage and proscenium arch were built. Chairs were borrowed from local undertakers to accommodate an audience of 130. From the workshop and rehearsal room on the second floor, scenery was moved to the third floor via a hand-pulled elevator.

Guild member Lloyd Taylor said, *"Later we obtained the space next to our rooms – an old gymnasium. We cut doors thru, built a stage (one foot high), bought 100 seats from the old Hippodrome Theatre, and were really in heaven."*

For two years, plays were presented here, a new play each month with three to ten performances of each. By this time, the charter group of 25 members had grown to 54. The Theatre Workshop was established where students trained and worked as apprentices under members of the Theatre. Young people, through schools and church dramatics, were encouraged to use the facilities of the Theatre and the technical knowledge of the staff.

According to Dorothy Jones, The Lakewood Little Theatre's (LLT) Women's Committee President, 1948-50:

> *"There was one small room on the second floor which they rented. Here they built their sets and transported them to the third floor where there was a small stage and auditorium. They gave a number of plays here and then they felt that they might be financially able to rent another room on the second floor. When this was done, they built their stage, but there were no seats. A committee was formed to see if they could locate any and with diligent search, they unearthed in the basement of the Hippodrome Theatre, 125 red plush seats which they purchased for fifty cents each. But another obstacle arose – they were not operating under the fire codes of the city – they would either have to build a fire door between the two rooms or move. They built a fire door. Things ran a little more smoothly for a while. A musical group of some 60 members had been added and another dream was being realized – that of giving Lakewood some of the Fine Arts culture it so richly deserved. Along with plays, concerts were being given and were well received."*

"People were so hungry for entertainment that they'd come to see the shows and they were always successful. And then, of course, came the dark period of television…" Helen Corns, Longtime LLT Actor and Volunteer, interviewed in 1994

"Working for a theatre gets in one's blood and there is no hope for release." Florence Elder, President of the Women's Committee, 1939

CHAPTER 5:
The Early Years of The Lakewood Little Theatre – 1933-1954

"I might digress here and tell how we came to incorporate when we did (in 1933)," said Lloyd Taylor. "We obtained Hayes (school) auditorium to play 'Craig's Wife.' (1931) We thought, since it was a depression and people were saving their gas we'd go to a neighborhood and they could walk to the theatre. The number 35 will always stick in my memory, because we charged 35 cents admission and just 35 people showed up."

"The result was we didn't have enough money to pay the royalty, but nearly two years later the publishers caught up with us and each of us whose name appeared in the program was threatened with a suit. We eventually settled a $1,000 suit for $300 and to protect our people, we incorporated under the name of The Lakewood Little Theatre."

Guild of Masques.

When "Mrs. Bumpstead-Leigh" is produced tonight and tomorrow by the Lakewood Guild of the Masques in its club rooms, 18519 Detroit Avenue, it will mark the second year of Lakewood's little theater group and also its second production since establishing a permanent headquarters.

Marguerite McGillis has been assigned one of the principal characterizations, supported by Lloyd Taylor, Vivien Weir, Don Glendenning, Evelyn Grove, Winifred Skyrme and others. Kathryn Kay is seen in the title role in the comedy by Harvey James Smith.

With a membership now of about 80 and a permanent little theater, where it plans to present a play each month, this group has taken rapid strides since it was organized only two years ago. Before then six or seven different dramatic groups existed in Lakewood, but all their careers were short-lived.

Then the Lakewood Junior Chamber of Commerce, feeling that dramatics have an important function in every community, appointed Richard Kay and a committee on drama to foster and sponsor little theater movement in Lakewood.

Began Career in Church.

The new guild's first production was given at the Evangelical Church at West 40th Street and Bridge Road. And from there the group moved to the Lakewood High School. Rehearsals had to be held at homes of the various members, often a play was staged without a dress rehearsal or without proper equipment in those days, but such things did not diminish the enthusiasm or ambitions of its members.

Versatility is necessary to belong to this organization. Under the supervision of William Kurz, for example, a crew of members designed settings and a portable stage within two days for the theater, which was formerly the Odd Fellows Hall.

Versatility is necessary to belong to this organization. Under the supervision of William Kurz, for example, a crew of members designed settings and a portable stage within two days for the theater, which was formerly the Odd Fellows Hall.

Two of the Guild's leading figures are Charles Robinson, director, who formerly was associated with the Montreal Little Theater, and James Henderson, art director. He previously has been a member of the Toledo Opera League, acted with the Strollers and Scarlet Masks Clubs at Ohio State, and trouped with the Players League as a makeup artist. Henderson not only paints the backdrops, makes posters and settings but also pinch-hits as a pianist at times.

Star Is Fashion Artist.

Kathryn Kay and Evelyn Grove, both fashion artists in Cleveland department stores, are also unusually active members, who aid Henderson. Richard Kay, the general manager, and a fluent pianist, worked for several years in English repertory companies. Mrs. Margaret Glendenning and Ida Gohr are assistant directors.

At present the Guild of the Masques is organizing a Junior Guild, for high school students, in which they will be trained in stagecraft, drama and acting.

Once a month a group of one-act plays are given to test the talents of new actors. If they give good accounts of themselves, they are promoted to minor roles in the regular productions. Somerset Maugham's "Constant Wife" and "Bill of Divorcement" are being tentatively considered by the Guild as their next offerings of the season.

THE LAKEWOOD LITTLE THEATRE

PRESENTS

"The Queen's Husband"

BY
ROBERT EMMET SHERWOOD

under the direction of
CHARLES ROBINSON

At The Theatre, 18517 Detroit Avenue

December 3, 4, 5, - 9, 10, 11, 1933
Curtain at 8:15

PRODUCED BY SPECIAL ARRANGEMENT WITH
LONGMANS, GREEN & CO.
NEW YORK

On May 12, 1933, the two-year-old Guild of the Masques incorporated into the not-for-profit arts organization The Lakewood Little Theatre, and the first production was a reprise of "The Queen's Husband" in December 1933. The following was included in its charter:

"The purposes for which said corporation is formed are: To promote and encourage the study and advancement of dramatic, musical and cultural art; to produce, exhibit and publish for private and public rendition dramatic performances, plays, compositions, music and paintings, together with other activities relating thereto."

The Dramatic School of The Lakewood Little Theatre opened in May of 1934, and Choral and Art divisions became active departments of the theater.

Plays were produced at the Little Theatre Workshop (Gormson's Hall), 18517 Detroit Avenue until December, 1934.

The Lakewood Little Theatre

18515 Detroit Avenue
Lakewood, Ohio

May 1, 1934

Dear Arvilla,

Monday evening, May 7th, 1934 will mark the opening of the Dramatic School of the Lakewood Little Theatre. This opening is only extended to the membership of the Theatre and will be so for the forthcoming summer term. By this it is possible to offer privileges to our own membership, which might prove difficult under other circumstances.

Classes are to be formed of not to exceed ten in number. Two courses are offered at this time, voice and pantomime. Either or both may be taken, each course consisting of ten lessons. Both may be taken simultaneously.

Mrs. Nungesser, the teacher, a graduate of the Curry School in Boston, Mass. has the cultural background, knowledge, and intelligence which the student body is bound to find beneficial.

The need of more definite and technical instruction to members of the Theatre, who aspire to stage work, is definitely evidenced. The need of a Dramatic School is essential to the community at large. Starting in a small way such as this, is our hope to establish, in Lakewood, a Curry Center which name has born itself admirably during the past decade.

Members who are desirous of participating in these classes should come prepared to register on the evening of May 7th, 1934, at 8 o'clock at the Theatre, 18515 Detroit Avenue. The tuition fee is $5.00 for each course, 50% of which is payable in advance, which you will readily recognize as a purely nominal amount. For further information you may refer to the writer or call Lakewood 4933 W.

With the sincere hope that you find it practical and possible to join one or both of the classes, we remain,

Cordially yours,

THE LAKEWOOD LITTLE THEATRE

Richard Kay

By   Richard Kay
     General Manager

May 1, 1934 - Letter from Richard Kay to LLT member

IS STARRED

Katheryn Kay, well known to patrons of Lakewood's Little Theater, is starring in the series of American Red Cross historical plays being broadcast over WHK each Monday evening at 7:30. Director of the productions is Richard Kay, her husband, and Steve Hazelwood, Republican club president and well known football official, is announcer.

CLEVELAND, (LAKEWOOD), OHIO, FRIDAY, NOVEMBER 16, 1

HUNDRED AT MEETING OF LITTLE THEATRE

About 100 members turned out to the regular monthly meeting of the Lakewood Little theatre last Monday night, which constituted the majority of the membership. The first part of the meeting was devoted to the discussion of plans for the future and the second part to entertainment and refreshments.

The theatre has extensive plans for the winter. Besides its regular productions they will be kept especially busy during the Christmas season of one-act plays and musicals for the various organizations throughout the city. Some of these plays are, of course, now ready, but others will soon be completed.

SUNDAY, NOVEMBER 18, 1934

From The Women's Board Scrapbook – 1934
The Lakewood Post and West Shore Post

Lakewood Elks Play Will Aid Needy Folk Here December 16

When Santa Claus stops his sleigh in Lakewood this year he'll find that he's had plenty of help and all he'll have to do will be to make his deliveries. The Lakewood Elks and the Lakewood Little Theatre have co-operated with him to give a Merry Christmas to the needy families of Lakewood and to aid them in their efforts they are asking Lakewood residents to come to "The Bellamy Trial" in the Elks auditorium on Dec. 16 and bring some sort of non-perishable food, such as canned goods, potatoes, flour, etc., for their ticket of admission. There will be a performance at 2:30 and one at 8:30. As will be remembered this play was given about a month ago. It enjoyed such success and had so many requests for a return that it was decided that it should be the means of giving Christmas cheer to Lakewood.

Besides being presented at the Elks Club it will also be given in the theatre's auditorium at 18517 Detroit avenue on Friday, Dec. 14. At this time the Junior League of Merrick House is taking over the house and all arrangements and ticket sales are being taken care of by them.

If it's excitement and suspense you like, don't miss this play. Who murdered Margot Bellamy? Well, come and see if the terse examinations of the district attorney will convince you or if you'll take sides with the attorney for the defense. You will see William Kurz, as the arrogant district attorney; Lloyd Taylor, the attorney for the defense; Kathryn Kay as Susan Ives, Ronald Skryme as Stephen Bellamy, Dorothy Bull as Mrs. Daniel Ives and their supporting cast of: Arthur Grove, Jerome Langell, Stephen Schmotzer, Robert Seibert, Dorothy Jones, Harold Innes, J. Browning Jones, Donald Glendenning, Ann Hemphill, Everett Erlinger, Harry Coopland, Jr., Walter Bull.

From The Women's Board Scrapbook – 1934 – Source unknown

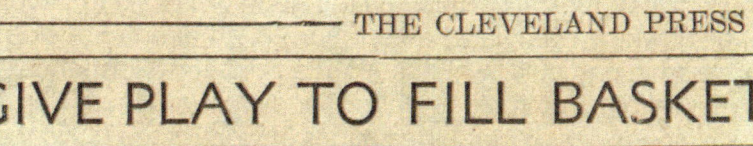

THE CLEVELAND PRESS

GIVE PLAY TO FILL BASKETS

Miss Comayns   Miss MacGillis   Miss Earley

Mr. Daltman   Mr. Kurz   Miss Phelan (seated)

Lakewood Little Theater Group, which recently was on radio programs in the Red Cross drive, and is prepared to produce several one-act plays for organizations throughout the city, will present "The Bellamy Trial," under the auspices of the Junior League of Merrick House Friday evening, Dec. 14, at the Little Theater, 18515 Detroit avenue, Lakewood. The show is given as a benefit for the Merrick House Junior League Christmas fund.

Leaders in the players' group, and in the Merrick House activities, shown in above group, are David Daltman, member of the cast; William Kurz, who takes the role of prosecuting attorney in the play; Misses Helen J. Comayns, Marguerite MacGillis and Elizabeth Earley, members of the cast; and Miss Helen Phelan, director of Merrick House.

From The Women's Board Scrapbook – 1934 – The Cleveland Press

31 | P a g e

From time to time, the various civic organizations had called upon the Guild to devote its services and present plays, all of which was gladly done, more in an effort to seek good will and public approval. One organization in particular which sought a benefit performance was the Lakewood Elks Club, when its Welfare Committee needed funds for its annual Christmas baskets. This organization was so impressed with the caliber of work of the Guild that it pledged its help at any time it was needed. When the Lakewood Fire Department declared Gormsan's Hall unfit for public gatherings, the Elks Club of Lakewood (under the guidance of Walter Quallish and Roy Daniels) offered use of their stage and auditorium citing The Lakewood Little Theatre's reputation for civic responsibility. During the preceding years, the group had given numerous benefit performances having served also on the Mayor's Committee for Relief of the Unemployed in Cleveland.

The Elks Club auditorium seated approximately 500. Other activities of the Elks organization restricted the LLT performances to Sundays exclusively. Sets had to be assembled at other locations and carried to the Elks Club in pieces. Local undertakers were called on to provide extra seats. Patrons were routinely turned away from sold-out shows. From 1935-1938, The Lakewood Little Theatre staged up to ten productions each season at the Elks Club. They performed a rich variety of quality drama to appreciative crowds and rave reviews.

The LLT was considered neither a club nor a social affair, but a civic project for all of the people of Lakewood and the adjacent suburbs. In 1934, the LLT became known for its radio dramatizations, including the story of the Red Cross and Clara Barton. During the Depression, local papers followed the company as it played for free to "vast armies of the unemployed" throughout Cuyahoga County.

In a letter from Social Activities Committee Chairman Harry Coopland, Jr. to LLT members dated September 12, 1934, he announced the first event – an evening of dancing, entertainment, bridge and refreshments on Saturday September 22, at 8:30pm. "You are assured that no factor will be overlooked which might contribute to a delightful evening. Tickets will be fifty cents a person and the Committee is arranging to furnish music of the highest quality obtainable."

Mrs. Olive Knirk – First President of The Women's Committee – Photo credit Beck Center

Several active and prominent Lakewood women felt that a Women's Committee should be organized to promote the aid and welfare of LLT. In February 1936, thirty-five women met at the home of Mrs. H. Louis Stettler to form a Women's Committee for The Lakewood Little Theatre, including Mrs. Olive (Carl F.) Knirk, Mrs. Carabella Johnson Schuster, and Mrs. Florence (Frederick) Elder. Mrs. Knirk became the president of the Women's Committee, and led the first subscription book drive for LLT. Establishing themselves as a formidable force in fundraising and subscription sales, the Committee boasted a closed membership of sixty women with an extensive waiting list.

"Times were different then," says Lee Mackey, wife of the late Artistic and Managing Director Karl Mackey. "We didn't have television, and the theatre

March 2, 1936

Form Lakewood Group To Aid Little Theater

BY DOROTHY HARMAN
Women's Club Editor of The News.

A NEW women's organization has been formed in Lakewood to help promote the Lakewood Little Theater movement, now in its sixth year.

. It is to be known as the Women's committee of the Lakewood Little Theater.

Definite plans have not been completed for the work of the women in the theater's promotion, but it is probable their activities will be similar to those in which the Women's Committee of the Play House takes part.

Mrs. Carl F. Knirk, widely known in Lakewood women's club circles, has been elected president of the organization and other members of the board include Mrs. Frederick Elder, secretary; Mrs. Edward C. Kahler, publicity chairman, and Mrs. H. Louis Stettler, chairman of the play-reading group.

The first play to be sponsored by the women is Philip Barry's "Holiday," to be presented Sunday at 8:15 p. m. in the Lakewood Elks club.

was quite important to everyone. People volunteered so much of their time and put such love into it." Indeed, the glamorous ladies of the Women's Committee were 1936's answer to television as the press reported on what they wore and where they vacationed. Famous for their sophisticated and floral themed fundraising teas, the ladies graciously opened their homes and welcomed the attention that ultimately led to more dollars for their cause.

Mrs. Elder felt the importance of having influential business men of the city helping the group. She took her enthusiasm to her husband Frederick L. Elder, and on October 21, 1937, twenty men met at the home of Mr. Elder. A Men's Advisory Board was organized under the leadership of Mr. Elder, Brice Bowman and John H. Anderson vice presidents, and Mr. L. E. Hackenberg secretary. The Advisory Board began with a total membership of 45 and later increased to 60 members. This group of prominent architects, engineers, and bankers began to search in earnest for a permanent venue.

Soon there were 60 members of the Women's Committee, 60 members of The Men's Advisory Board, and about 100 members of LLT itself who were each expected to sell at least 10 subscription books per season at $5 each.

The Lakewood Little Theatre had recognized the necessity to not depend solely upon one person, but to have efficient personnel trained to fill in for one another's jobs. Richard Kay, general manager and dramatic director, for three years a member of the staff of one of the largest theaters in England, had experience acting, a practical knowledge of play production and its relevant problems as both an artistic and business venture. Mr. Kay had also completed courses of training of The Leland Powers School of the Spoken Word in Boston, Massachusetts. He had for the previous two years been President and a trustee of The Ohio Theatre Conference, an association of the outstanding Little Theatre and Dramatic Groups within the State of Ohio. This Conference was formed at the insistence of the drama department of Western Reserve University and made financially possible through the Rockefeller Foundation. Mr. Kay was an industrial engineer in everyday life, and the Senior Partner of one of Cleveland's leading firms of public accountants.

In 1937, the Theatre staff consisted of three assistant Dramatic Directors each qualified to produce plays and to give dramatic instruction: Catherine Marwitz Stettler, J. Browning Jones, and Florence Nungesser. Technical Director Robert H. Seibert was one of the charter member of the Guild of the Masques and had a great deal of practical experience. President William Kurz was Associate Technical Director, having had over ten years' experience at the Bay Village Players, Bay Village, Ohio. He studied play production under Mr. Kay and had been an observer in many of the eastern little theatres. A delegate to the Ohio Theatre Conference, he was frequently called upon as a consultant by dramatic groups in Greater Cleveland and its vicinity on technical problems.

Classes in voice and diction, pantomime, and scenic design were open to members of The LLT free of charge. A registration fee was required which was refunded upon attendance to 85% of the offered hours of class and laboratory instruction. A course was also offered to advanced students in the Art of Play Production, instruction being given by Mr. Kay.

Public tryouts were held prior to every major production. Non-members of the Theatre were allowed to perform in one production, and should they wish to continue to participate in plays, they were required to become a member. As indicated in the Code of Regulations, there were various types of membership in the Theatre. The entire membership fluctuated between 7 and 150, but the nucleus of staff remained constant.

Execution of business matters was under control of Mr. Oliver T. Nungesser who also served as the Theatre's representative to the Lakewood Elks Club. All publicity releases were cleared through Mr. Gilbert Knight – Chairman of the Publicity Committee of the Men's Advisory Board, with exception of the Women's Committee publicity which was routed through the Society Columns.

It was difficult to earn enough revenue to make any profit. In a written history by an unknown author in 1937, "We do not make as much profit as we might because the scenery cost is burdened on one performance, whereas that cost would not increase for fifty other performances of the same show. We are forced to pay the maximum royalties, whereas if we continued to present the same show, the royalties would be exceedingly reduced on successive performances."

In addition, revenue suffered when audience members were faced with the following:
- Limited seating capacity
- Uncomfortable seating
- Level floor, making it difficult for those further back to see the stage
- Many people objected to attending "amusements" on Sundays only
- Box office not accessible enough ahead of performances

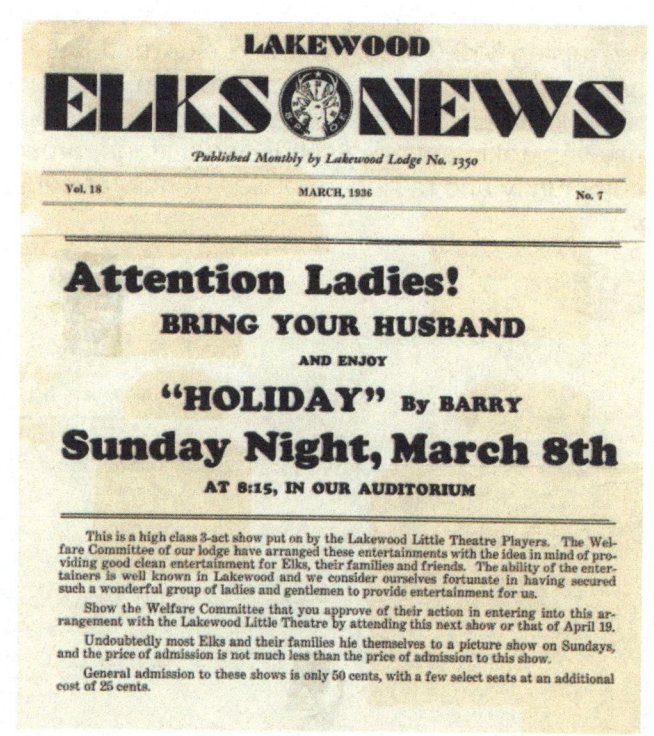

March 1936 – Lakewood Elks News

The Lucier Motion Picture Theatre at 17823 Detroit Avenue became available for lease with an eventual option to buy. When it was leased by LLT in 1936, there was on-site parking at the rear of the stores on the easterly side of the theater. A driveway was adjacent to the east side of the building. Because the theater needed space for set construction and storage, a group of volunteers from the Men's Board worked with home builder Peter Kleist to build at the rear of the parking lot a structure which formed a wall of the passage from the lobby over to what is, as of 2022, the Studio Theater and Dance Studio.

The plan was for LLT to produce one performance before the close of the 1937-1938 season (May of 1938), and then start early in September of 1938 with ten different shows for the 1938-39 season, each to run at least for six consecutive performances, this would enable the group to give 61 performances.

The location of the Lucier was ideal at the west end of Detroit Avenue; many of the Theatre patrons and volunteers resided in Clifton Park, Rocky River, and Bay Village. It was a central point of the suburbs and convenient to Parma, Berea and southern suburbs from which patrons also came.

The presence of motion picture houses did not concern the leaders of the LLT, since the audiences were thought to be entirely different from that of the little theaters. There were numerous schools in the Cleveland area engaged in teaching dramatics, but a "Theatre" school had more appeal to prospective students because they had the opportunity at all times to participate in the regular Little Theatre productions, thereby making their studies more effective.

The fact that the Lucier was in need of extensive and costly renovations was no obstacle. Despite the Great Depression, the members of the Women's and Men's Committees set the goal of raising $10,000 to give The Lakewood Little Theatre its first genuine home. These men, to name a few, engineer John H. Anderson, architect Edward Conrad, business administrators Brice Bowman and Gilbert H. Knight, did not hire out the work to be done. They remodeled it themselves, taking out seats, building a stage, proscenium, and dressing rooms, going out to the community and raising necessary funds for equipment.

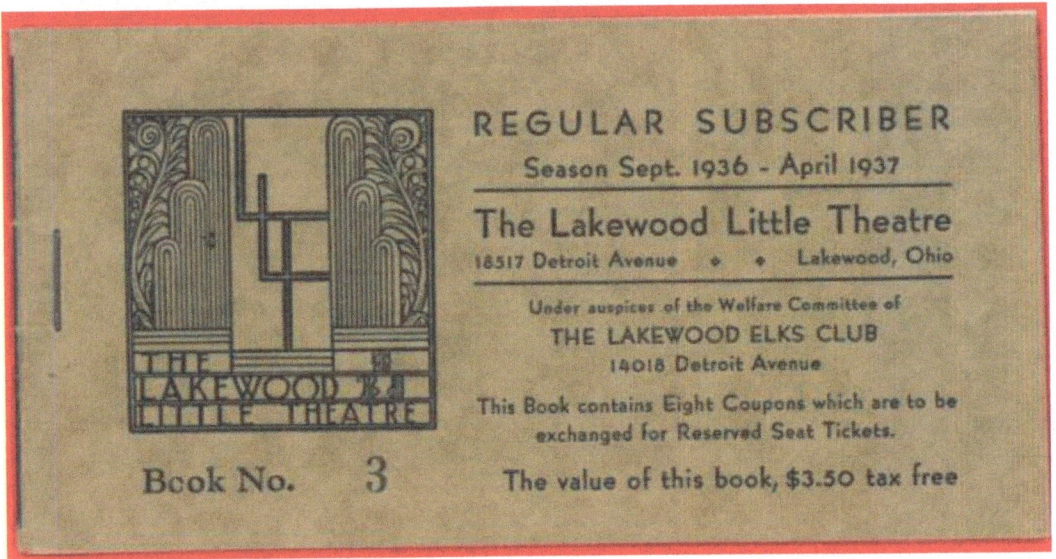

April 24, 1938 – The Lakewood Little Theater hits "Big Time"
© 1938 The Plain Dealer. All rights reserved. REPRINTED/USED with permission.

In January of 1938, the Board of The Lakewood Little Theatre was enlarged by amendment of its Code of Regulations from seven members to thirteen, to provide for the following:

- The President and two others members of the Women's Committee shall be elected to the Board of Trustees
- The President and the two Vice-Presidents of the Men's Advisory Board shall be elected to the Board of Trustees
- Thus, it will be observed that an effective control of the three major units of the "Theatre" are coordinated, making for a common ground on which each division may express its ideas as a normal and proper function.

On May 7, 1938, the Tulip Teas and tireless subscription drives paid off. That evening, the curtain rose on The Lakewood Little Theatre's first production in its renovated home. Hollywood openings had nothing on LLT's first night. Flash bulbs flashed and drama critics of all the major Cleveland newspapers were there. The sold-out crowd of black-tied and top-hatted dignitaries enjoyed Fred Ballard's "Ladies of the Jury" on a beautifully lit, 46-foot stage. Acknowledging that the theater had struggled for eight years against nearly insurmountable odds, Mayor Amos I. Kauffman declared it "Lakewood Little Theatre Week." His formal proclamation stated that "The appreciation and development of the drama is a fine and essential activity in any well rounded community."

A four-page "history" of LLT was written in 1938 for the grand opening of their newly renovated space in the Lucier Movie Theatre: *"The present period of readjustment, following the World War, has shown a tendency to breed a materialistic spirit which is so alien to the Arts. The useful encourages itself, but without understanding or appreciation it would be fairly impossible for the Fine Arts to outlive utilitarian efficiency."*

Proclamation

Being of the opinion that the appreciation and development of the drama is a fine and essential activity in any well rounded community, and recognizing the achievements of the Lakewood Little Theater, in its earnest efforts during the past eight years to develop a democratic appreciation of the best in the theatre, which efforts are now to be crowned by the opening of their own beautiful building, I, the Mayor of Lakewood, officially proclaim May 7 to May 14 as Lakewood Little Theatre Week.

It is my hope that during this time the aims and ideals of the Lakewood Little Theatre may be called to the attention of the people of Lakewood, so that they may be inspired to support this movement which means so much to the civic and cultural development of our beautiful city. Every one is invited to become a supporter and part of the Little Theatre, the sole purpose of which is to promote the arts, entertain the public, provide an outlet for artistic expression, and develop talent which might otherwise remain unrecognized.

AMOS I. KAUFFMAN,
MAYOR OF LAKEWOOD.

1938 proclamation which appeared on the first page of the commemorative opening night playbill

EVELAND PLAIN DEALER, SUNDAY, MAY 8, 1938

New Stage Makes Lakewood Bow

LAKEWOOD GREETS LITTLE THEATER

Capacity House Goes Formal for Opening

BY DAVID L. RIMMEL

Lakewood put on its best bib and tucker last night and, with more swank than that suburb has seen at any municipal event of recent years, gave the Lakewood Little Theater a rousing sendoff in its new home at 17823 Detroit Avenue.

Enjoying its top-hatted and evening-slippered role of first nighter was a capacity audience, composed largely of civic and city officials, many of whom had served on the committees which made possible a

The attractive new stage of the Lakewood Little Theater was a court room for the opening of the dramatic groups first permanent home last night.

permanent house for the eight-year-old dramatic group.

The formally dressed patrons who filed past a reception committee of wide-eyed neighborhood children found a theater which, inside, had little resemblence to the double-feature neighborhood house which had a long suburban history under the name Lucier.

Externally the Little Theater was familiar, except that removal of display cases had revealed a simple brick doorway. The interior was a compact, neatly furnished auditorium, nicely suited to the needs of a little theater organization.

Remodeling Cost $10,000

Demodeling had cost $10,000, Richard Kay, general manager and dramatic director, announced from the stage. The results were a 50-foot stage, well lighted and tied to the auditorium by a short flight of steps which ran the length of the stage.

The stage was hung with plain, harmonizing drapes of gray and of rose — which theater attaches insist is raspberry au lait (raspberry and milk). The color scheme was carried through in lighting fixtures of the same rose shade and gray walls.

The deepened stage had been installed at the cost of a number of rows of seats, reducing the seating capacity to 465, almost by half of the former motion picture house.

Burtons on Hand

Mayor Harold H. Burton and Mrs. Burton represented Cleveland at the event, and Mayor Burton was the first to be introduced in the brief ceremony which preceded the opening performance.

"We admit that Lakewood is a good place in which to live," Mayor Burton said to the audience, "but this makes it still better."

Kay related the work of the women's committee and men's advisory board of the theater, introducing many of the leaders in the two groups and others of the Little Theater movement. Among those he presented before turning the ceremony over to Mayor Amos I. Kauffman of Lakewood were Mrs. Carl F. Knirk and Mrs. Frederick L. Elder, president and vice president, respectively, of the women's committee, and Elder, president of the men's board.

Kauffman, honorary chairman of the board, introduced officials of neighboring suburbs, whom he invited to return often with the residents of their municipalities. Introduced were Mayor and Mrs. L. O. Bean of Strongsville, Mayor Roland E. Reichert of Parma, Mayor and Mrs. E. E. Campbell of Dover, Mayor and Mrs. Merl Weiger of Bay Village, Mayor and Mrs. Louis Mares of Brook Park, Mayor and Mrs. George Spaulding of Olmsted Falls, Councilman and Mrs. George A. Metzger of Rocky River and N. C. Cotabish, mayor of Lakewood in 1910 and 1911.

Cuts Curtain Ribbon

To the Lakewood mayor fell the honor of cutting the ribbon which allowed the curtains to open on the court room setting of Fred Ballard's three-act comedy, "Ladies of the Jury," which, with its genial complications, half-a-dozen accents and catch-lines, such as "The lawyers aren't obliged to tell the truth, the whole truth and nothing but the truth," had the Lakewoodites chuckling through much of the performance.

The opening production will be shown until May 20 with reserved seats but with the requirement of formal attire eliminated.

Among bouquets on display in the lobby were two from the Shaker Players and the South Euclid Little Theater, wishing success to the first West Side "Play House."

Lakewood Opens New Little Theater With Murder Play

Lakewood's officials and sponsors of Lakewood's Little Theater are making Saturday a civic celebration when the eight-year-old organization baptizes its new headquarters in the remodeled Lucier Theater at 17823 Detroit Avenue with "Ladies of the Jury."

Mayor Burton and Mayor Amos I. Kaufman will cut the ribbon, while ten other West Side mayors will join in the ceremonies. Remodeled at an estimated cost of $12,000, the theater has 465 seats, a 46-foot stage, a modern lighting system costing $1,800 and is decorated in live gray and rose colors.

"Ladies of the Jury," the group's first subscription play here, is a popular Broadway court room melodrama by Fred Ballard. It centers around an ex-"Follies" girl, played by Jean Doyle, on trial for the murder of her elderly and plutocratic husband. H. Louis Stettler, jr., portrays the judge.

Kathryn Kay will appear as the society woman who is called into jury service, a role created by Mrs. Fiske and later assumed by Edna May Oliver on the screen. The other jury members are Arvilla Quayle, DeLene Stover, Ida Belle Jacobs, Vera Traxler, Hilda Robinson, William Jurz, Carl A. Grulke, Otto A. Spieth, J. Browning Jones, Jay L. Ward and Steve Schmotzer.

Richard Kay is directing the group, which also includes Lloyd R. Taylor, Gordon Klein, John Lan- dis, John Traxler, Ferne-Beverly Jones, Doris Herold and Ray Enright. Beginning May 7, the melodrama will run through May 20.

KATHRYN KAY

H. LOUIS STETTLER, JR.

1938

At Lakewood's Opening

Herewith you have Bill Robert's impression of the opening of Lakewood's new Little Theater, which took place on Saturday evening with suitable garnishings. For their first effort the players selected Fred Ballard's amusing comedy, "Ladies of the Jury," which was brought to the stage under the direction of Richard Kay and will continue until May 20.

Lakewood Players Open New Theater

Capacity Crowd Greets Group's First Show, "Ladies of the Jury"

With appropriate fanfare the Lakewood Little Theater's impressive new home was thrown open to the public over the week-end with a capacity first-night audience of various dignitaries, including Mayor Harold Burton and his wife, An and Kaufman, mayor of Lakewood, and various other people woun... have been long interested in the venture.

As their first vehicle this group selected Fred Ballard's comedy, "Ladies of the Jury," which was originally seen on Broadway with Mrs. Flake in the leading role and later was given a screen treatment by Hollywood with Edna Mae Oliver as the star. The plot, briefly, describes a woman on trial for murdering her husband and almost all of the action takes place in the Jury Room.

The first ballot brings in a vote of 11 to one for conviction—the dissenting juror being an extremely strong-willed woman who is convinced the accused is innocent. It then becomes her business to convince the others their viewpoints are in error and her methods not only give the play its vitality, but bring most of the cast to nerves edge and the breaking point. The role is played by Kathryn Kay with assurance, charm and authority.

For that matter the entire cast struggles valiantly with their roles and altogether the results are gratifying and rather unexpected—especially considering the entire company are amateurs of practically no experience at all.

The theater itself is handsome, has been carefully and well decorated and should bring new and added interest to Lakewood's civic activities. The production will continue, incidentally, until May 20.— W. F.

1938 – Cleveland Press

Within days, Cleveland papers were splashed with headlines touting the Theatre's great success. In its first week alone, LLT had already drawn 2,265 patrons. Far from resting on its laurels, the company planned an ambitious succession of seasons featuring new shows nearly every six weeks. Auditions often attracted up to three hundred aspiring artists. The Women's Committee continued its tradition of selling subscriptions over sumptuous teas, while the Men's Board raised cash and painted sets.

In 1938, approximately 15 children were enrolled in classes at $10/year, receiving training each Saturday morning. And on October 20, 1938, Articles of Incorporation were filed by Richard

Kay, Jay L. Ward, and William Kurz, for Lakewood School of the Theater, with a principal office located at 1145 Union Commerce Building in Cleveland.

Filed

Oct. 20th, 19 38

No. 174935

STATE OF OHIO.

ARTICLES OF INCORPORATION

—OF—

LAKEWOOD SCHOOL OF THE THEATER

The undersigned, a majority of whom are citizens of the United States, desiring to form a corporation, not for profit, under the General Corporation Act of Ohio, do hereby certify:

FIRST. The name of said corporation shall be ___Lakewood School of the Theater___

SECOND. The place in this State where the principal office of the corporation is to be located is Lakewood 1145 Union Commerce Bldg., Cleveland _____ Cuyahoga _____ County.

THIRD. The purpose or purposes for which said corporation is formed are:

To conduct and operate an educational institution for the purpose of teaching the dramatic arts and correlated subjects.

IN WITNESS WHEREOF, We have hereunto subscribed our names, this ___10th___ day of ___October___, 19 38

Richard Kay

Jay L. Ward

William Kurz

THE STATE OF OHIO, COUNTY OF ___CUYAHOGA___, ss.:

Personally appeared before me, the undersigned, a Notary Public, in and for said county, this ___10th___ day of ___October___, 19 38 the above named ___Richard Kay, Jay L. Ward___ and ___William Kurz___, who each severally acknowledged the signing of the foregoing articles of incorporation to be his free act and deed, for the uses and purposes therein mentioned.

WITNESS my hand and official seal on the day and year last aforesaid.

SEAL

Frank P. Celeste

Notary Public.

United States of America ⎱
STATE OF OHIO ⎰ ss.
Office of the Secretary of State

I, **William J. Kennedy,** Secretary of State, of the State of Ohio, do hereby certify that the foregoing is an exemplified copy, carefully compared by me with the original record now in my official custody as Secretary of State, and found to be true and correct, of the Articles of Incorporation of _____

LAKEWOOD SCHOOL OF THE THEATER

filed in this office on the ___20th___ day of ___October___, 19 38, and recorded in Volume ___455___, Page ___421___, of the Records of Incorporations.

WITNESS my hand and official seal at Columbus, Ohio, this ___20th___ day of ___October___ 19 38

William J. Kennedy

Secretary of State.

October 10, 1938 – Articles of Incorporation, Lakewood School of the Theater

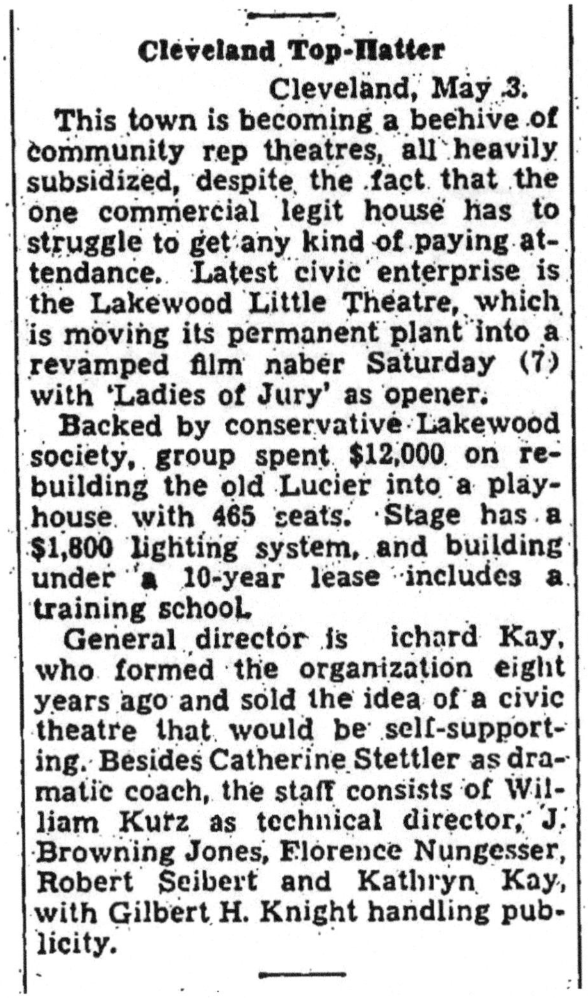

Cleveland Top-Hatter

Cleveland, May 3.

This town is becoming a beehive of community rep theatres, all heavily subsidized, despite the fact that the one commercial legit house has to struggle to get any kind of paying attendance. Latest civic enterprise is the Lakewood Little Theatre, which is moving its permanent plant into a revamped film naber Saturday (7) with 'Ladies of Jury' as opener.

Backed by conservative Lakewood society, group spent $12,000 on rebuilding the old Lucier into a playhouse with 465 seats. Stage has a $1,800 lighting system, and building under a 10-year lease includes a training school.

General director is ichard Kay, who formed the organization eight years ago and sold the idea of a civic theatre that would be self-supporting. Besides Catherine Stettler as dramatic coach, the staff consists of William Kurz as technical director, J. Browning Jones, Florence Nungesser, Robert Seibert and Kathryn Kay, with Gilbert H. Knight handling publicity.

May 4, 1938 Variety

From the occupancy of only the theater space in 1938, the group expanded activities to the point where by the mid-1950s, it occupied half of the former commercial store space on the ground level and the largest of the six apartments on the second floor. These areas were given over to a spacious, beautifully furnished lounge (just east of the lobby), quarters for the children's and adult's schools, and a large office where clerical work and mailing was done.

August 2, 1939 – Cleveland Memory Project

Theater classes continued to evolve, and an article in the Cleveland News, September 20, 1939 announced, *"The Lakewood School of the Theater sponsored by The Lakewood Little Theatre opens its second season September 18, retaining their class rooms of last year at 15620 Detroit Avenue. Mr. Kay, president of the school announces the appointment of Mrs. Carl F. (Olive) Knirk as Managing Director of the School and also announces the addition of Mrs. Harriet Hughes Snider, well known as a teacher of Voice and Diction in Cleveland, as a member of the faculty staff. The School will offer day-time classes for students of the school age in a general dramatic training and adult evening classes in Voice and Diction, Stage Technique and allied subjects."*

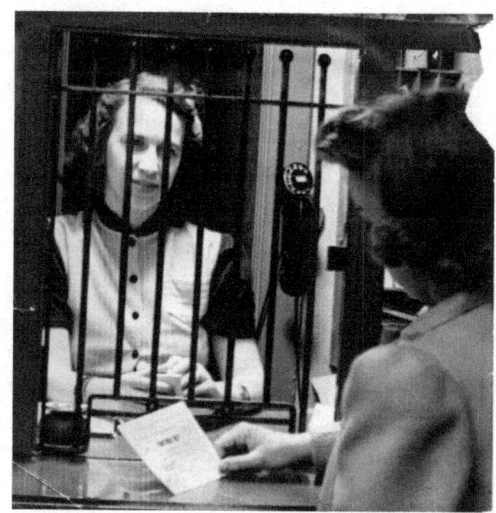

"Mrs. J. B. Jones" – first box office employee 1938-1940

THE OLD BOX OFFICE

1940 Box Office Crew (L to R) Jean Revilock, Betty Spilker, Helen Doethlaff
Photo credit: "B. F. Denly Studio, 1150 West 3rd St, Cherry 0634"

Room Service playbill – 1938-1939 season

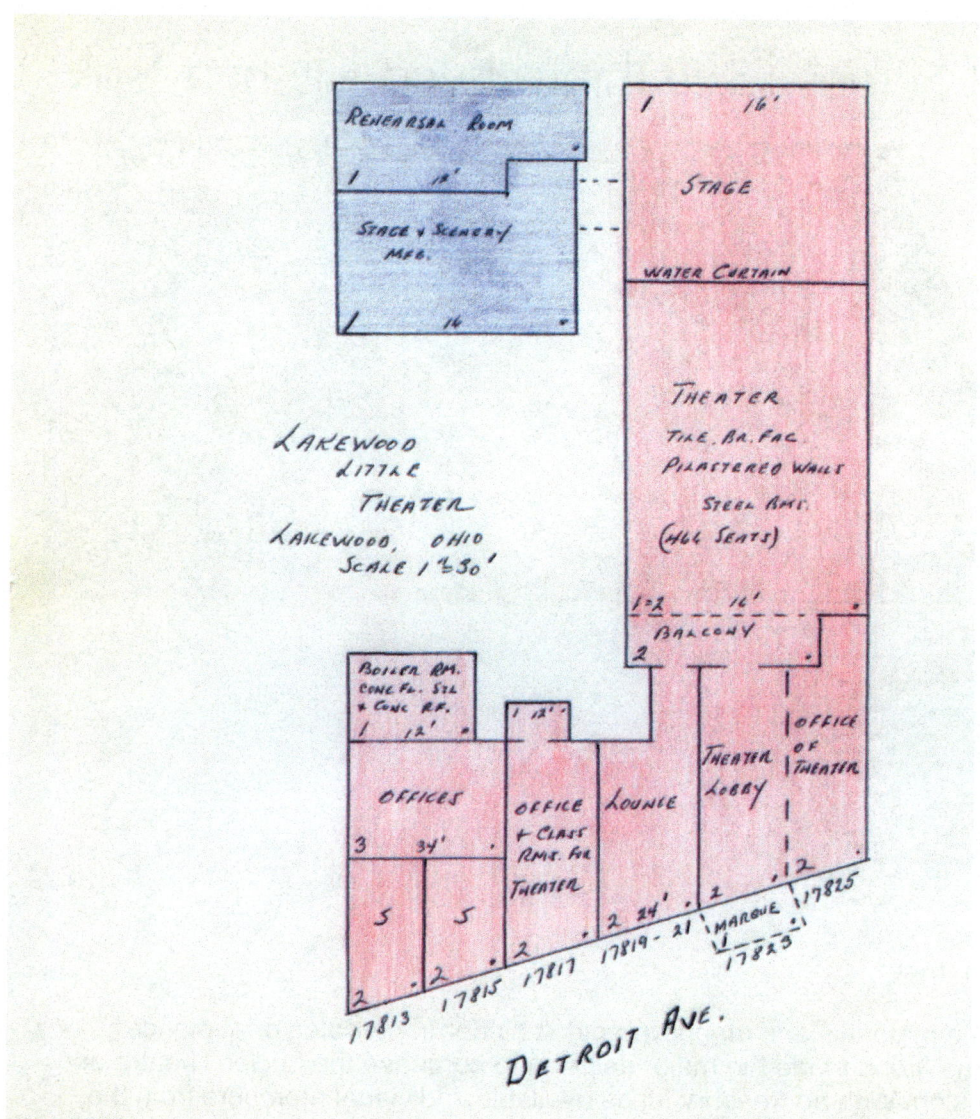

Unknown date

Nothing could stop them. But in 1941 war was declared and many young men left to fight for their country. In 1942, director Richard Kay who had been the guiding light was called to service and became an officer in the United States Navy. The Women's Committee devoted October of 1942 to sponsoring a massive scrap metal drive in the theater lobby. Calling for all of Lakewood to donate their "luxury scrap metal," the Committee's popular slogan read "Heirlooms and knickknacks of the past will make planes, ships and ammunitions for the future of America." The theater began doing plays which called for more women, and the community understood.

Lakewood Scraps Everything—Even Kitchen Sink

THE Luxury Scrap Metal Drive now in progress at the Lakewood Little Theater under the direction of the Women's Committee is bringing in a wide variety of articles."

Everything, including the kitchen sink, has been turned in. One member gave a dinner party and entertained the guests by allowing them to break up two old ice boxes and trudge to the theater with the zinc. Miss Elsie Muth, and her sister, Lena Muth of Clifton Boulevard, turned in an heirloom brass and copper stein, 75 years old, belonging to their grandfather, who received it from the owner of the old Muth Brewery.

Photographed with some of the collection were (left to right): Mrs. Lawrence Hackenberg, 13810 Lake Avenue, with the stein turned in by the Muth sisters. Mrs. Vernon Roberts, 1267 Thoreau Road, and Mrs. Wilson Selner, 20560 Erie Road, as they weighed a metal bread basket. Mrs. Carl E. Heil, 17439 Lake Avenue, chairman of the drive, surrounded with aluminum pots and pans. Mrs. Gordon Klein, 1243 W. Clifton Boulevard, and Mrs. Frederick Elder, 17411 Edgewater Drive, lugging a basket of brass and copper (Mrs. Elder is carrying her own donation of a metal cocktail shaker).

October 13, 1942 Cleveland News

The shortage of wartime materials and manpower didn't hinder ticket sales or audience enthusiasm. In 1944, the group made the major decision to purchase the Lucier Theatre and began talking of expansion. With no treasury funds available, individual members from the Men's and Women's Boards, based solely on their dedication and hope for the future, signed personal notes for a total of $5,000 to acquire a land contract agreement. This later made it possible to obtain a $50,000 mortgage (which through income generated from box office receipts and rentals, was paid off in 1957 with great celebration).

In a 1994 interview with actor and LLT volunteer Nick Brodella, he recalled LLT shows during the 1940s: *"Well, there's 'Laura,' 'Junior Miss,' and we also did things like 'Mr. and Mrs. North,' which was a very popular murder mystery comedy at the time, and if you read it today, you almost gag. But that was then...We did a show called 'Dark Tower,' and this was at the time when the veterans were just coming back from fighting the Second World War, and they had discovered culture over in Europe. And we were – no matter what we did here – we were packing them in. And this 'Dark Tower' was a show that started at 8:30pm and wasn't over until 11:30-11:45pm, and packed them in, and they sat there and ate it up. And it really wasn't a very good play…*

…I lived in Cleveland. I had to get here using two streetcars and a bus…We did a show called 'Junior Miss' which had a lot of teenagers in the show. Teenage comedies right after the war were very popular. And we hit a blizzard, and by God, with my two streetcars and a bus, I made

it. One of the other actors could not get here, it was absolutely impossible, so we went on and I had to do his part, and just on the spur of the moment think how to change the lines because the other part was like a macho football player, and I was playing a more, shall we say, wimpy college student."

Pages from The Women's Committee Scrapbook - 1945

The first full-time, paid managing director – Gordon Klein – was engaged prior to the opening of the 1946-47 season and he remained until 1949. A full-time technical director was retained in 1947. Before this time, dramatic directors had been hired and paid on a per show basis. The large crew of volunteer technicians continued to operate under the direction of the full-time managing director and technical director.

Bramer Carlson became director in 1949 and was replaced in 1952 by Clay Franklin who directed the group for one season. Guest directors were also hired for the 1952-53 season and Betty Piper was executive producer. Karl Mackey became the managing director on August 1, 1954.

Mrs. Lovejoy, Mrs. Berkey and Mrs. Jones

Mrs. Dorn and Mrs. Becker

Mrs. Wilson, Richard Overmyer and Richard Jr.

Women's Committee Boosts Lakewood Little Theater

BY FRANCES SNYDER

Lakewood's Little Theater's 17-year-old Women's Committee has a well co-ordinated band of chairmen whose favorite project is promoting the theater and its productions.

Working together to make it a success, their teamwork is the antithesis of the theater's season sign-off—"Every Man for Himself," June 4-21.

An important rule is played by the clerical committee. Guided by Mrs. J. Brewning Jones, clerical committee chairman, its members staple, address and prepare for mailing bulletins which for each production run well into the thousands. Always on hand to do their stint are Mrs. Meldrum W. Berkey, president, and Mrs. Roger E. Lovejoy.

month, is already setting its sight on the subscriber-membership campaign it will help launch August 1. With a $12,000 building program, now under way to provide a rehearsal stage and space for new building, to make the theater one of the cultural centers in the community, the group plans to expand its scope of activities and add new members to its roster.

L.L.T. Women Sponsor Pot Luck Supper

Women's committee of Lakewood Little theater, will hold a potluck picnic at 12:30 p. m. Tuesday at Clifton Beach. After a brief business meeting, Mrs.

CLEVELAND PLAIN DEALER, MONDAY, JUNE

VITAL STATISTICS on the books for Lakewood Little Theater women's committee: It's the fifth child and second boy at the Harvey F. Neil's. John's the newcomer's name. . . . Mrs. Hamilton W. Watt has dubbed her month-old gentleman Hamilton Wesley Watt Jr. . . . Mrs. Edwin Killear houseguesting Mr. and Mrs. George Keith and Malcolm of Derby, England. She's Mrs. K's sister-in-law, tickled pink with the United States and hoping to stay.

And that's what I know about women!

LAKEWO

May 1947 – Cleveland News

During the 1947-1948 season, a workshop and rehearsal hall were built adjacent to the theater, making possible rehearsals and set construction for the next show while the current show was in progress.

In 1948, 4,000 subscription books were sold. In a 1994 interview, longtime LLT actor and volunteer Helen Corns looked back on that time saying, *"The Men's Board, the Women's Board, and the Drama Production Wing were all in competition – who was going to sell the most books. We'd have a prize. We'd have all these things for incentives. While the War was on, nylons were still in short supply, and so was meat. One of the first prizes was a ham. Another one of the first prizes was nylon stockings. Those were some of the incentives for selling books in those days."*

1948 – Mrs. Oliver Nungesser, LLT Pantomime Director and Robert Corns, actor reminiscing as they sort old plays – photo credit Beck Center

Mrs. Oliver Nungesser
Robert Corns

Also in the 1947-1948 season, the Drama Production Wing of the theater was formed. This was a separate organization within the theater composed entirely of backstage and technical personnel who worked on the LLT shows. Highly skilled professionals from nearly every vocation were represented.

Having achieved one seemingly impossible dream, The Lakewood Little Theatre became determined to carry their passion for drama beyond producing plays. Their vision for the future involved providing theater education to the community's youth.

Furthering the evolution of theater classes and the Lakewood School of the Theatre that was incorporated in 1938, The Lakewood Little Theatre School arrived in 1948 with actress Virginia Woodworth as its first director. Classes for beginning and advanced students were offered for students aged four through high school. All aspects of stagecraft and a wide variety of classes were offered to shape creativity, encourage self-confidence, discipline and provide basic techniques of the stage. Classes for adults were offered in acting and stand-up comedy. (approx. 800/year in 2002)

Mrs. Woodworth recruited the original teaching staff. Among the first hires, was radio talk show personality, "Lady Jan" Egert. Mrs. Egert said that the program had a clear purpose from the very beginning. *"Our focus was not on creating child stars. The objective was always to teach children to be more comfortable with the spoken word so that they could become better in school and in life. I was thrilled to be involved."* This culture of focusing on the individual has persisted throughout the decades.

In a 1994 interview, Mrs. Egert recalled the following:

"In 1948, Howard Egert is in "Philadelphia Story. He had lived in Philadelphia, but he was not a lawyer then. He was an engineer and then he went to law school. He decided he wanted to follow in his father's footsteps (Howard H. Egert), and he went to law school and became an attorney, and that's when I met him – when he was going through law school.

He put himself through law school by doing commercials remote, early commercials at WEWS downtown when he would pour the POC (Pilsener Brewing Company) beer. You couldn't do it on camera in those days, and then they would go back to the ball field and he was paid very nicely for that. If we hadn't met here at The Lakewood Little Theatre, we would have met at WEWS because I too was doing commercials – Coca Cola commercials – where they simply handed me a bottle of Coke and said 'talk about it.'... In 1949, on January 8th, there was a note in the paper that new classes were to begin in speech at Children's Theatre. Now, that suggests that there might have been a hiatus or that this was an expansion in their curriculum.

We actually started in 1948, and there had been because of the early war years, there was no children's theatre here to my knowledge. I came in 1948 from radio station WJW and Virginia Woodworth started all this. We started with eighty students, and we are now registering close to eight hundred (1994)... Virginia Woodworth was supervisor and Dorothy Sanders and I provided 'guidance' – that was the word that was used...I was hired as radio/television director here and we did shows. We did the classics downtown at radio station WJW which the theatre arranged, and we had our rehearsals down there so all these students auditioned for roles on the radio...

Virginia Woodworth knew my mother and father and she kind of kept track of what I was doing. She realized when I was out of college that I had the TV knowledge and radio and speech and script work, and that was what she was hoping to fill in 1948 on her staff. So she called, and it was that easy. She was a very interesting person. Virginia Woodworth had a great knowledge of the stage and she put together a wonderful program. Her father was a newspaper editor in Fostoria, and she was thin and wiry and so full of energy that it was like an egg beater going through a room. But she knew what she wanted to do, and she wanted children to become comfortable with the spoken word and that's where I came in. It has to begin in their childhood. You have to become comfortable with the spoken word or as adults we are not able to describe how we feel or what we think, and so the program came together very nicely...

We are one of the few children's theatres that uses children on stage. Mostly the shows that you see downtown or around for children, adults are doing the acting. The Lakewood Little Theatre has always used children for the acting and the production of these shows, and we're one of the few that has maintained this over the years, and we're still doing it...

Our school goes beyond that in helping the child build self-confidence...Our aim is not at our auditions to look for the prettiest little girl or the darlingest little boy. Our aim is to look for the person who can handle the part, handle the lines, and we're not center-stage-oriented here...Lots of talented children come through here and they have to learn to share the spotlight with the not-so-talented and the ones that are having trouble with the spoken word. There is a lot of creativity in children that has to be brought out and the schools don't have time anymore to do this...

I retired in 1988, just short of forty consecutive years of service."

Cleveland Shopping News – Sept 28, 1953

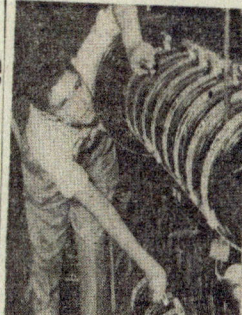

Youngsters Perform, Manage Stage in Progressive Children's Theatre

(Pictures on page 1)

WHEN the curtain is raised on a children's play at the Lakewood Little Theatre, small hands are behind the scenes flipping light switches, sounding doorbells and telephones and manipulating stage props. This flourishing children's group which helps develop potential Broadway actors, also concentrates on teaching future directors and set designers the elements of stagecraft.

The theatre, now beginning its fourth season of working with young people from six to 16 years old, conducts classes in voice, diction, make-up and sound projection. Every detail of their semiannual productions from acting to curtain raising is handled by youthful members. Outside of introducing children to the theatre, the fascinating work helps shy youngsters develop poise and confidence, says Mrs. Dorothy Sander, director of the group.

Gladly Give Up Movies

Approximately 100 are enrolled each season, with the majority falling into the 9 to 14 age bracket. Many have been with the theatre for the full four years and usually by the time they have finished their second year, are avid theatre members who have no regrets about giving up Saturday football games or afternoon movies.

Classes are held each Saturday morning with children arranged according to their experience. Mrs. Sander is assisted by Mrs. Jan Egert, Mrs. Sally Finan and Mrs. Helen Bennett who alternate the instruction. When a new play is started, rehearsals are held each afternoon after school. Unlike most young groups, the children have the use of the complete facilities of the adult theatre.

All parts in the plays are double cast as insurance against measles, mumps or broken arms that may hold up the schedule. Children alternate in their roles for the five performances usually given in January and June.

Make-Up Like Professionals

Each performer has his own make-up kit and after a few lessons can apply a basic make-up of foundation, rouge, lipstick and eyeshadow like a professional. Older children study more extensive character make-up.

The honor group of the theatre is the Maskers Club to which children are elected after they have

Bill Albertson, 1597 Elmwood ave., stands ready to manipulate the lighting panel as the curtain raises on a theatre play.

appeared in two or more plays and participated in backstage activities. Members hold a formal initiation and award pins. The name of the club which the theatre hopes will eventually designate the entire children's section, was the title used by the adults 25 years ago.

Several children each year try their full-fledged stage wings in juvenile roles of the adult productions. Three of them appeared last season in "The Happy Time."

Another large segment of the theatre activity is the radio and television classes which set up panel discussions on timely topics such as wearing lipstick in school, problems of dating and current events. They hope to transport their discussions to a local radio station sometime this fall.

Like most theatre groups, they often have trouble filling male roles. Boys are somewhat reluctant to become actors until they have observed a few sessions. The next production, "Little Women," which probably took that factor into consideration, will open in January.

In the Pictures, Page 1:
1. With the aid of a tape recorder, members of the Lakewood Little Theatre radio classes check their presentation. Ronald Marks, 3405 W. 159 st., follows the script as Virginia Teare, 16500 Edgewater dr., broadcasts. Director Dorothy Sander watches proceedings.
2. Grease paint and acting go hand in hand. Instructor Sally Finan assists Virginia Gold, 3125 W. 139 st., with her eyebrows while Claudia Bobey, 14618 Rainbow dr., practices.
3. In the backstage workshop, Deanne Albertson, 1597 Elmwood and Jim Slovensky, 2135 Wascana ave., build flats for a new production.
4. A nice rounded O helps clear up indistinct diction. Instructor Helen Bennett demonstrates the pear-shaped tones to Kristine Caster, 27501 Butternut ridge and Linda Johnston, 1673 Mars ave., in the theatre's voice classes.

In a "School Report for 1952-1953," Chairman of the School Committee Olive Knirk reported, *"In the three years The Lakewood Little Theatre School has been in operation it has steadily grown in size and in efficiency. This year closed with an enrollment of 101 boys and girls ranging in age from 6 to 14 years. Dorothy Sander was again the Director and was ably assisted by Helen Bennett, Mona McCormick and Betty Piper….At the end of the first semester, the School produced "The Little Princess," a very colorful and beautifully costumed show. At the end of the second semester, we gave "Tom Sawyer." The costumes for both shows were made by Irma Kolben of The Lakewood Costume Shop, next door to the Theatre. We gave five performances of each show and each show was double cast. The double casting serves two purposes. It gives a double set of children the opportunity of stage appearance and secondly if a child in one cast gets measles or mumps, there is someone trained to take his place."*

June 1953 LLT School Flyer

"One time, Karl went up to the stage to make a point to an actor (passionately), and pounded the stage so hard that he broke his hand," recalls former Technical Director Don McBride.

CHAPTER 6
Evolution of Education Programming and the Karl Mackey Years 1954-86

In August 1954, Karl A. Mackey became the artistic and managing director of The Lakewood Little Theatre. Born in August 1924 in Cleveland Ohio, he was a graduate of Lincoln High School, received a BA degree in Dramatic Arts from Western Reserve University in 1949 and a Master's degree in Dramatic Arts from Western Reserve University in 1950. He had directed at Cleveland College and guest directed three productions at LLT in 1953-1954 before being named managing director.

With Mr. Mackey at the helm, classes included instruction in basic theater techniques, diction, and characterization. He and his wife Lee who volunteered in all aspects of the theater, made it all happen at The Lakewood Little Theatre. He made sure that Saturday mornings belonged to the children, entrusting them with use of the stage, lighting, and sound booths. Parents immediately pitched in and became an integral part of the activities, helping out with everything from costumes to fundraising. The students performed two plays each year in those days.

In a 1994 interview with Lee Mackey, conducted by long-time volunteer Lee Ann Curry, Mrs. Mackey recalled:

> *"Karl was dedicated to that theatre and he did whatever he had to do with whatever time he had to do it in. It was a job that he felt totally dedicated to. So I did everything I could; I sold season books, I did mailings with the Women's Board, which was all done by volunteers. I helped the Women's Board in their rummage sales. I was a member of DPW (Drama Production Wing). As a matter of fact, I was kind of a representative of Karl's in the DPW because he didn't have time to go to all the meetings. So, I went and expressed concerns that DPW had that weren't important enough to take to the Board of Trustees... We took our daughter Lisa there when she was born...*

> *...We took Lisa to the theatre a lot because we didn't have a babysitter that much. But when she was little, teeny tiny, it didn't really matter that much, as long as she was being taken care of... When she was going to school I would bring her less, but she would also come after school with us to the theatre. I once asked her, 'How did you feel that we weren't always at home and Daddy didn't always come home?' And she said, 'You know, Daddy was always reachable by phone.' She said, 'Now if you're asking me if I think I had a normal life – that was normal for me. Whatever you guys were doing, that was normal for me. And I loved going to the theatre. I loved staying at rehearsals. I loved listening to Dad give notes. I just loved it!' And she also helped. When she grew older, she did lights, she worked in the prop room, she worked everywhere...*

> *...And now Lisa produces TV and radio commercials for an advertising agency. She has done that. As a matter of fact, her theatre experience, like when she finally started to act and do lights and learn about directing, helped her an awful lot in her job now."*

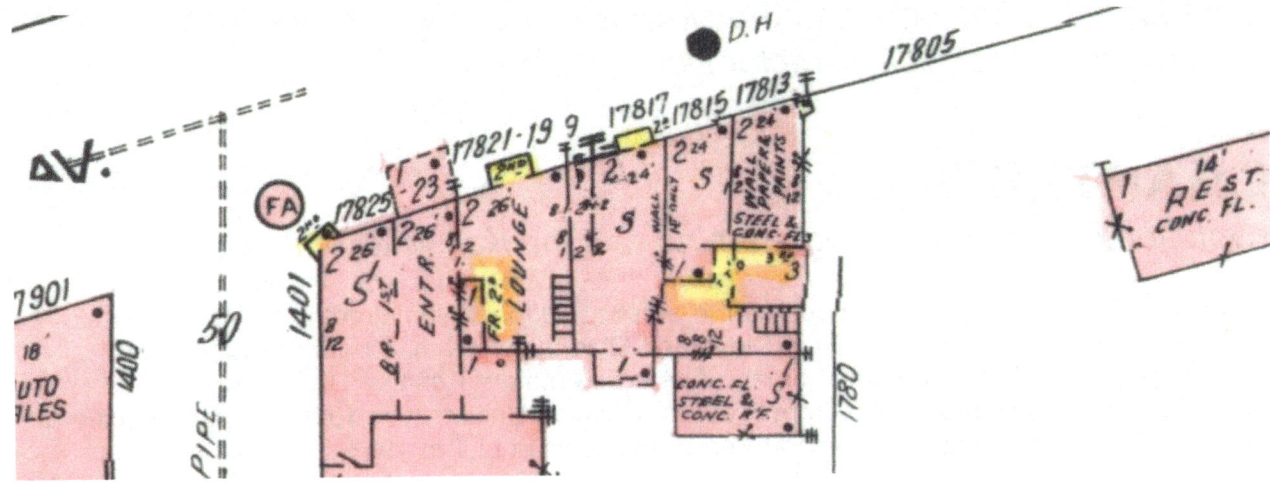

From County records 1952

In 1958, The Lakewood Little Theatre Fine Arts Foundation was established to administer the Theatre's long-term investments. The Foundation's stated purpose was to develop a new Cultural Arts Center, a dream of the Trustees since the 1940s, and more specific planning began which explored the scope and range a center might one day possess. After investigating many sites in the west shore area, a feasibility study in 1963 showed that remaining in the present location seemed to present the best opportunity because of the considerable assets already acquired and the convenient accessibility of the location.

Additional land area was needed and a program of land acquisition was undertaken, beginning with the parking lot east of the theater. This property cost $100,000, and as houses in the immediate area went on the market, they were acquired, using revenues from the theater operation.

Ross Ellis, who had attended Guild of the Masques meetings, took time off to raise his family during the late 1930s and 40s, but became active in the early 1950s with the Men's Board of LLT and became President in the early 1960s. He commented, *"By that time, the growth had made it necessary to search for more parking space to meet the demands of the increased number of patrons. Because of my activities as a Real Estate Broker, I was asked to serve on a site selection committee to study the possibilities of finding a location where a new theatre could be built that would house not only a stage but a full-fledged cultural center. This committee drew upon such citizens as Mayor Frank Celeste, Developers Peter Kleist and George Seltzer, Architect Fred Toguchi, Attorney Wallace Heiser, and others. As the search continued, it became obvious that the location on Detroit Avenue near Wayne was a very good one and the decision was made to stay there."*

In 1963, growth continued. The Theatre purchased 28,000 square feet of parking lot space for $100,000. The resurfaced lot brought the entire estimated value of the property to $250,000. For several years, expansion came in small steps as the Theatre gradually acquired surrounding storefronts, lots, and several apartments above the building. The addition of a rehearsal hall and classroom was followed by new central air conditioning and heating systems.

1963-1964 season

Intermission - Time for a ghost story!

People often ask about ghosts in theaters. There was no mention of any in the archives except for this story, from a 1994 interview with Andy Kosiorek (technical theater volunteer):

"In the early 1960s, there was a volunteer named Paul, and he met his wife at the theater. They married and were killed in a plane crash on their honeymoon in Europe. They were well regarded by many people. Paul was primarily in the technical area of the theater and their death really had an impact on many people. A couple of things were dedicated to them in the old theater. And so when sometimes something would go bump in the dark, people would say it was his ghost."

Back to youth theater education…

By 1962, "Teen Theatre" had been established to accommodate the needs of older students who wished to remain in the program.

And then in 1964, Lynda Sackett[4] began teaching dance in the Children's Theatre and choreographing student productions. In a 1994 interview, Ms. Sackett recalls, *"My sister was*

---

[4] Lynda Sackett's long connection to the organization began with her role in The Lakewood Little Theatre's production *Seven Year Itch* in 1964, and soon after that, she started teaching dance in the children's theater classes. In 1975, she approached Artistic Director Karl Mackey with a 26-page proposal for a Dance Education program. They promoted it in the fall of 1975 and opened in January 1976 with 200 people in the beginner classes, M-F. Her passion for dance and for the arts led Ms. Sackett to be even more involved with Beck Center, serving as both Director of Outreach Education and Director of Visual Arts Education, while continuing the dance program. She received the Ohio Dance Award for Excellence in Dance Education in 2000, and the Arts Outreach Award as Distinguished Educator in 2003. Ms. Sackett established the educational culture of Beck Center – caring about the growth and education of the whole person, rather than encouraging students to compete against each other. Although she retired as Director of Dance Education in November, 2007, she remained at Beck Center as a part-time dance faculty member until her full retirement in June, 2019. On the occasion of her partial retirement in 2007, generous supporters made contributions to establish the Lynda Sackett Endowment for Dance Education, and many continue to give to the fund every year, in support of the dance program.

involved with our Children's Theatre and The Lakewood Little Theatre; Susan Harris, who later went on to California and became a member of the Screen Actors Guild (SAG-AFTRA). She encouraged me to try out for a play, 'The Seven Year Itch.' I auditioned and, of course, Karl Mackey had never seen me before in his life, and he cast me as the French girl. I had a fabulous time being in the production. I thought Karl was wonderful, and Cliff Donnelly was in the production with me. I told him that I had a dancing school, and he had seen me practicing. As it turned out, he was then, for that year, head of the Children's Theatre. And so, he called and said would I consider teaching as part of the Children's Theatre? And I said yes, that I would. So, I joined the Children's Theatre, and Cliff moved to California, and Jan Egert returned. I think she had probably been on a sabbatical for that year, and she returned as my wonderful Director. She really was a gem to work for. I become the choreographer for the Children's Theatre and taught Saturday mornings for a period of ten years…

Corner of Detroit and Wayne Avenues – mid-late 1960s – Cleveland Memory Project

Examples of current Beck Center values have been consistently demonstrated since the start of LLT. Children's Theatre faculty always went "the extra mile" in support of the students. Children's Theatre alumni from productions in 1968-73 still have letters from their director Barbara Anne Swearingen praising their performances. Mrs. Swearingen was the regional auditioner for the American Academy of Dramatic Arts.

The desire to engage children in the arts has always been paramount, since ultimately, in lifelong learning, the arts can be transformative and strengthening for individuals and their communities. The following example from 1965 shows that the Children's Theatre program was "…designed to develop and shape the creativity of young people…to teach self-discipline…handle themselves well in all phases of life."

CHILDREN'S THEATRE
REGISTRATION
SATURDAY, SEPTEMBER 11, 1965
9:30 a.m. until 12:00 p.m. in the Lounge
Classes begin September 25

TO THE PARENTS ABOUT OUR SCHOOL . . .

A part of the Lakewood Little Theatre, the Children's Theatre School is designed to develop and shape the creativity of children and young people, to teach the self-discipline needed for real art, and to provide the basic techniques of the stage.

COURSE OF TRAINING INCLUDES: A continuous curriculum composed of four major levels. Level I emphasises the mechanics of acting, Level II the physical, Level III the mental and Level IV the emotional aspects of the theatre.

The major goal at all levels is to extend and develop the voice, diction, body control and general poise. Students of the theatre school are expected to express and handle themselves well in all phases of life.

CLASSES: Saturday mornings, 9:30 - 11:00 for children under 12. For those 12 and older, classes are 11:00 to 12:30.

SCHOOL TERM: September 25 to December 11 is the first semester; February 5 to May 7 is the second semester. Vacations according to Lakewood Public Schools schedule.

TUITION: Twenty dollars per semester. If additional children in the same family register, their tuition is reduced to fifteen dollars per semester. When students are cast in plays a fee is charged for costumes, scripts, and makeup.

STAFF: Director, Clifford Donley; Helen Bennett, Mary Morgan, Holly Hollister, James Keiser, Mary Kay Strasek.

PLAYS: Two are produced annually. Dates for the first production are January 15, 16, 21, 22, and 23. Plays are cast from members of the Theatre School on the basis of teacher recommendation, a reading, and rightness for the part.

TEEN THEATRE: Monday evenings, 7:00 to 8:30 p.m. Offering advanced work in all phases of the theatre to students 16 through 20 years of age. Students are given opportunity to produce studio shows and are eligible to participate in major Theatre School Productions.

Registration: Monday, September 20 and 27, 7:00 to 8:00 p.m. Classes begin October 4. Tuition is $20.00.

LAKEWOOD LITTLE THEATRE
Children's Theatre
17823 Detroit Ave.   LAkewood 1-2540

September 11, 1965 – Children's Theatre Registration

INFORMATION

Registration for Children's Theatre School, Spring Semester:

SATURDAY, FEBRUARY 8, 1969

In the Theatre Lobby from 10:00 A.M. 'till Noon
Tuition: $20.00 per Semester
Classes: Begin February 15, 1969

Students, Age 6 thru 10 — 9:30 to 11:00 A.M.
Students, Age 11 thru 15 — 11:00 to 12:30 P.M.

(For further information, call the Registrar, Mrs. Spilker at LA 1-2540)

☆ ☆ ☆

LLT CHILDREN'S THEATRE SCHOOL

The school is organized into four levels of training:

Level One, the beginning students learn stage habits and traditions.

Level Two emphasizes body movement or physical in acting.

Level Three emphasizes the mental in acting, characterization and diction.

Level Four emphasizes the emotional, taking advanced students as far as they are capable of going in acting.

The LLT Children's School is dedicated at all levels to the improved poise, self-control, and speech of its students, which will be useful in all phases of their lives. Director: Jan Egert.

APPRENTICE THEATRE

Classes held Saturday afternoon, 2:00 P.M. to 4:00 P.M. for graduates of Children's School, plus newcomers 16 years or older. Students will be given the opportunity to study and participate in the total production picture: sound, lighting, costumes, set design, in addition to advanced study of acting techniques. Registration and tuition — same as Children's Theatre. Classes begin Saturday, February 15, 1969. Director: Mary Morgan.

Twentieth Season
1968 - 1969

Lakewood Little Theatre Children's School

presents

"THE SNOW QUEEN"

Directed by Barbara Ann Swearingen
Choreography by Lynda Sackett
Settings by Russ Rissman

Friday, January 24	8:00 p.m.
Saturday, January 25	1:00 and 3:30 p.m.
Sunday, January 26	2:00 p.m.
Friday, January 31	8:00 p.m.
Saturday, February 1	1:00 and 3:30 p.m.
Sunday, February 2	2:00 p.m.

LAKEWOOD LITTLE THEATRE

17823 DETROIT AVENUE   LAkewood 1-2540

Box Office Open Monday through Saturday,
2:00 P.M. to 9:00 P.M.

All Seats Reserved: $1.00

1968-1969 Lakewood Little Theatre Children's School Playbill – "The Snow Queen"

1967-68 Thespia Awards – Laura Davidian, Paul Orgill, Karen Jordan, Bernard Singerman – photo credit Beck Center

An extensive 1969 remodeling project improved audience seating and increased space for the growing Children's Theatre and scenery work. The educational programs were expanded with the introduction of art classes in 1969.

LLT Premiere Night Offers 'Red Carpet' to Drama Patrons

Lakewood Little Theatre's "Cinderella transformation" opens to the public Saturday night, Sept. 27, for "Premiere Night."

Meantime there's a committee picking its way carefully through the scaffolding and other remodeling equipment, as members meet there to plan Premiere Night.

The gala opens at 7:30 that night with a punch bowl reception. Theater-goers literally will get the red carpet treatment—klieg lights, doormen and even someone ready to park cars for guests.

IT'S ALL a benefit honoring LLT's 40th anniversary. Forty is a key number. A handful of people paid just 40 cents 40 years ago to attend the first production, "The Queen's Husband," by Robert E. Sherwood.

Theater goers at this premiere will see Woody Allen's comedy, "Don't Drink the Water." Curtain time is 8:15 p.m.

To round out the evening, guests may go on to the

RICHARD COAKWELL, chairman of the LLT new seat fund; Russ Rissman, technical director and Andrew Matthews, maintenance chief, admiring contrast between old and new theater seats.

(Sun photos by Harry Newell)

Westlake Hotel Ballroom for a buffet and dancing to Frank Strasek's orchestra.

Mrs. Leslie Robblee heads the premiere night committee-Mmes. William Wiese, Richard Coakwell, Charles Purdum, George Pipik, Helen Sack and Carol James.

DESIGNING decorations for Premiere Night are Russ Risman, technical director of LLT, and Mmes. Robert London, Morris Eller and Charles Swearingen.

Theater improvements which were made possible by donations, include air conditioning, new seats, carpet and lighting, and new sightlines done by elevation. Seats still may be purchased for $100 with the name of the purchaser inscribed on a brass plaque.

Premiere Night is open to the public. Reserve by calling the theatre box office.

LEE (MRS. KARL) MACKEY, Mrs. William Wiese, Karl Mackey, who is beginning his 16th year as LLT director, and Mrs. Leslie Robblee, premiere Night chairman.

In a 1994 interview with Karl Mackey, he recalled a story about the carpeting that was installed in 1969:

> "Frederick Dorn lived on Lake Avenue in a French Provincial house. He had the corner lot on Whipporwill. Subsequently, there's been a house built on that corner, but Fredrick Dorn was re-carpeting his house, so he said to me, 'Karl would you like this carpeting?' and I went over there to look at it, and it was green carpeting, and I said yes we would love to have it, and so we got the carpeting from Fred Dorn's house. He was President of Ohio Savings, and we carpeted the inner lobby, the aisles, and across the front row in front of the stage with Fred Dorn's carpeting. Years later when we took over some of the apartments upstairs, we carpeted those halls up there with the same green carpeting…
>
> … Greenly and Hess remodeled the front of the building once, back in the fifties. Roy did the sketches for us and we covered the old coal bin windows across the front… Back in

1957, the storm damaged our marquee and when we had to redo it. The marquee had been almost out to the curb line, and a truck coming down Detroit hit that marquee, so we had to have it set back away from the curb line and the whole front of the theatre was redone at that time. That had to be late fifties, early sixties...

...I like those basements downstairs. Nobody gets to see them but it's very interesting how they all connect underneath. Originally, each store had a separate stairway down to their section of the basement, and it still may be there in the old check room which is now the pottery shop, a trap door there with a stair going down. There is a stair from the Wayne Avenue apartment entrance down to the basements. When I first went there, all the costumes were in the basement. They were on the floor. There was a big wooden crate affair they built that must have been about twenty-five feet long and about eight to nine feet wide and the costumes apparently had been hanging in there at one time and now they were all on the floor...

...The props were in the next room, and so we took the room under the lobby which was a very dry room and made that into a costume room, and I guess the prop room we put under the pottery shop. The bamboo shop had a basement that was under the room next to the lounge, east of the lounge and so when he left, he left a lot of good shelving down in that basement, so that is what we used for our prop room which later then became the children's theatre costume prop room."

LLT used every space available for its programming, and yet always tried to accommodate additional demands on the use of the spaces. Free meeting space was provided to the Playwright's Theatre during the 1980's, to help local writers develop new plays. On May 8, 1970, disaster struck The Huntington Playhouse in Bay Village when it was destroyed by a fire. A schedule of musicals had been planned for the summer, and when Bud Binns and Marty Schickler, co-operators of Huntington approached Karl Mackey, he and the Board of Directors were sympathetic and agreed to allow the use of the LLT facilities for production of their season. Thanks to LLT, the season successfully opened on July 1, right after the close of LLT's 40th season on June 6, 1970.

1968-1969 season

Between 1958 and 1974, the Theatre acquired all of the Detroit Avenue frontage between Wayne and Rockway Avenues and six dwellings on these streets. An agreement was made with the Ohio National Guard so that the Theatre could acquire an 80 foot strip of the northern end of the Armory property providing a total land area of approximately 2 and 1/3 acres. It was on this site that the Kenneth C. Beck Center for the Cultural Arts would be built.

"I never dreamed I could be this happy!" – Ken Beck

CHAPTER 7:
Enter Kenneth C. Beck – A Man with a Dream (The Development of Beck Center for the Arts, 1972-1999)

In February 1972, Artistic and Managing Director Karl Mackey received a phone call from then Lakewood Mayor Robert Lawther who told him of a gentleman who wished to remain anonymous, who was interested in leaving his estate to the city so that it could build a museum in Lakewood Park. "Kenneth Beck[5] came in one day to discuss leaving one million dollars to the City of Lakewood to build an art museum," said then Mayor Lawther. "He said he was a retired millionaire and at first I wasn't sure whether he was serious. But when I was finally convinced he meant business, I put him in touch with Karl Mackey to discuss financing the Little Theatre's expansion."

In a 1994 interview with Robert Lawther (then Judge Lawther), he said,
> "I was Mayor of Lakewood from 1964 to 1976... I was in the office one afternoon when my secretary came in, said a gentleman wanted to see me, and she ushered him in, and he said 'I'm Ken Beck.' I had never seen him before; his clothes were very rumpled, and he needed a shave. I thought, 'OK, I'm here to talk to the public.' He said, 'I'll come right to the point. I want to leave a million dollars to the City of Lakewood to build an art museum in my memory in Lakewood Park.' You can imagine what I thought about that from a total stranger.
>
> After an hour, I was convinced he had a million dollars and he told me his whole story. He had been a window dresser at Sterling Lindner Davis. After World War II, he made a lot of money in the stock market in the fifties which is when you could make money if you knew what you were doing. He said he had been around the world seven times, never married but knew lots of women. He obviously was very eccentric, was an amateur artist. He had this money. He had offered it to some city in Florida and they didn't know if they were interested or not, but he was from Lakewood and he thought he would like to leave it to Lakewood for an art museum. I thought, I have to handle this guy pretty carefully. I said Lakewood Park doesn't have room for something like that. There's not enough parking now, and if you stop to think if you build a museum for a million dollars, who is going to maintain it, where is the money going to come from? Well, he said, the

---

[5] A native of Indiana, Kenneth C. Beck arrived in Cleveland in January 1915 to enroll in the Cleveland School of Art. During that first year, he attended the school for one term, but then became much more interested in engaging in city life. A job in a sign shop led to a career in window displays and ultimately his own printing business which became involved with the Chicago World's Fair. In the years prior to WWII, his company became the fifth largest manufacturer of exhibits and displays in the US. Realizing that the impending war would curtail his business, he sold out and retired at the age of 46, often traveling the world studying and collecting art, and always returning to his condo in Lakewood Ohio until his death in 1977. Everywhere he traveled he painted the local scenes and collected artifacts. Never married, Mr. Beck continued to study art during his retirement. When illness forced him to winter in Florida, he took lessons from renowned water color artist Eliot O'Hara. With over 200 watercolors on hand, Mr. Beck chose not to sell his art, but instead donated paintings to friends and charities in Northeast Ohio.

city could do that, and I said the city doesn't have the funds for that kind of thing. It's all we can do to put police and firemen on the street.

So after at least an hour, I'm thinking very rapidly, I said what you need is some established organization that would take this money and use it wisely and administer it and make sure that it meant something after you're gone. Because we were talking about inheritance then. So I mentioned Lakewood Little Theatre and he fluffed that off very quickly. He didn't have very high regard for it. He didn't know that much about it, but he didn't think of that as a very outstanding art situation. We talked further and I knew and told him that they had plans to build a new theatre and were looking for finance to do it, and this might be a wonderful opportunity to provide some seed money when the time came to really get the project off the ground. Well, he didn't say no, but he wasn't terribly interested, but he said he would think about it…

The time came when he got interested in doing something during his lifetime. He finally offered Lakewood Little Theatre $300,000 to help get this project off the ground. I think the project was going to cost about a million and a half to build this new building and they had a big dinner his honor to announce this gift. As I recall, Karl Mackey was up introducing him, telling the story of how they had worked with him and had these plans, and Mr. Beck has kindly offered to donate $300,000 right now to get it off the ground. Ken Beck was there smiling and having a good time. He pulled on Karl's sleeve and said, 'Make it $600,000.' That is my recollection. He doubled the gift right there at the dinner."

Mayor Lawther told Mr. Mackey that he informed the gentleman about the Lakewood Little Theatre and of the fact that they had for years been working to try to create a cultural center for the arts. Some weeks later, Mr. Mackey received a phone call from Attorney John Cannell, and he supplied some information about the current conditions of LLT and future planning.

A few months later in the fall of 1972, Mr. Cannell again called Mr. Mackey, this time asking how the plans were coming. When Mr. Mackey professed that he didn't know he was to have prepared any schematics, Mr. Cannell suggested that it would be a good time to bring his client – Kenneth Beck – up to date by visiting him in Florida and taking along a schematic and rendering that would show Mr. Beck the potential scope of the proposed center. In a 1994 interview with Howard Egert (Lakewood Little Theatre's longest-time Board President, 1965-1977), Mr. Egert recalled, "Karl went to Florida to see Mr. Beck, and he did a great job. He sold the deal…Mr. Beck was mainly interested in the museum. He was not really interested in the theatre."

Mr. Mackey talked to Mr. Beck along with his attorney John Cannell several times before he agreed to support the Theatre's plans to build a multi-cultural arts center. "In the end Mr. Beck was very impressed with the way we did business," says Lee Mackey. "He believed in doing everything on his own and respected that the Little Theatre operated the same way."

Mr. Egert recalled, "When I told (Ken Beck) about the tax saving feature; making the gift right now, during his lifetime, and the great tax saving he would realize, and avoiding capital gains and everything else, and he said, 'Well fine. Let me think it over.' So, he apparently talked to the people at Internal Revenue, to see if what I told him was true. He called me one day and said 'When can we do this?' I said, 'Fine.' So, I called Bob Corns and we went down with Ken Beck to The Cleveland Trust Company where Bob was Special Record Officer, and he pulled out a block of Roadway Express stock which he had paid $4,500 for and which was now worth*

$320,000…And he said 'Here it is' and signed it over, and we sent it to the broker and sold it the same day."

In the meantime, theater and education programming kept going strong, and in particular the opening of the theater season was as grand an event as it had ever been.

1973 Premiere Night (L to R) Guest Director Frank Zelesnik, Helen Corns, Janet Egert

1973 – Photo credit Bill Plotz

Interstate 90 in Lakewood, then known as "the road to nowhere" – an unfinished eight-lane superhighway at what would become the McKinley Avenue ramp – became a spectacular destination on September 15, 1973, when the traditional season opening party literally "went on the road." Chairs Bob and Lee Ann Curry had read an article suggesting that some use should be found for the unfinished and yet-to-be used highway. After calling and writing state officials for about six weeks, they got permission from the Ohio Department of Transportation. With tables topped with umbrellas, flaming torches, and barrels topped with flowers, actors in white ties and tails filled glasses and popped corks all evening. "I knew it wasn't going to rain," said Ms. Curry, "It just couldn't." The crowd then got onto double-decker buses and went to the theater to see "The Roar of the Greasepaint and the Smell of the Crowd," and then to Wagner's Country Inn for a midnight brunch and dancing.

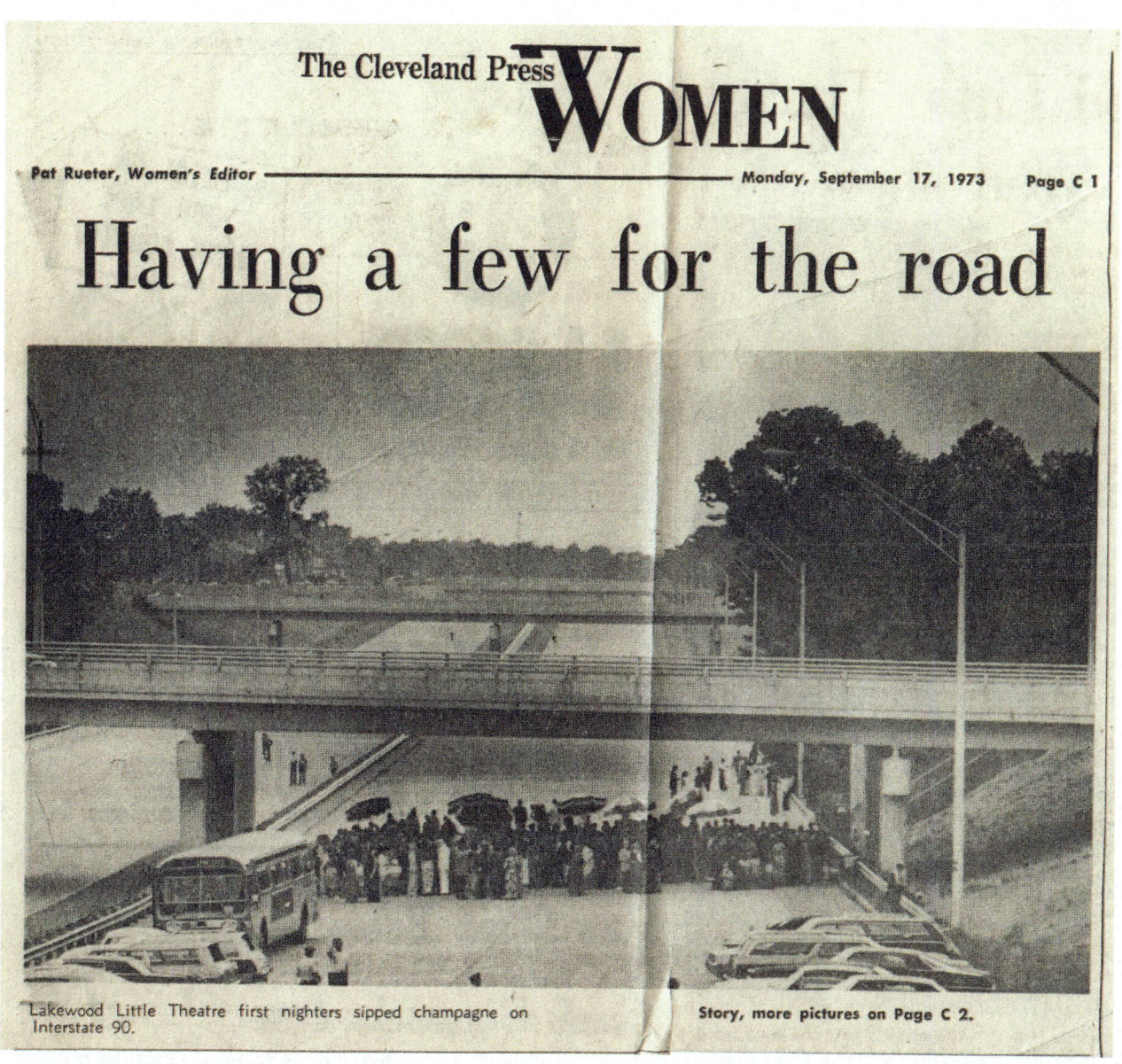

The Cleveland Press **WOMEN**

Pat Rueter, Women's Editor ———————————————— Monday, September 17, 1973   Page C 1

Having a few for the road

Lakewood Little Theatre first nighters sipped champagne on Interstate 90.

Story, more pictures on Page C 2.

September 17, 1973 The Cleveland Press

Freeway will be party site

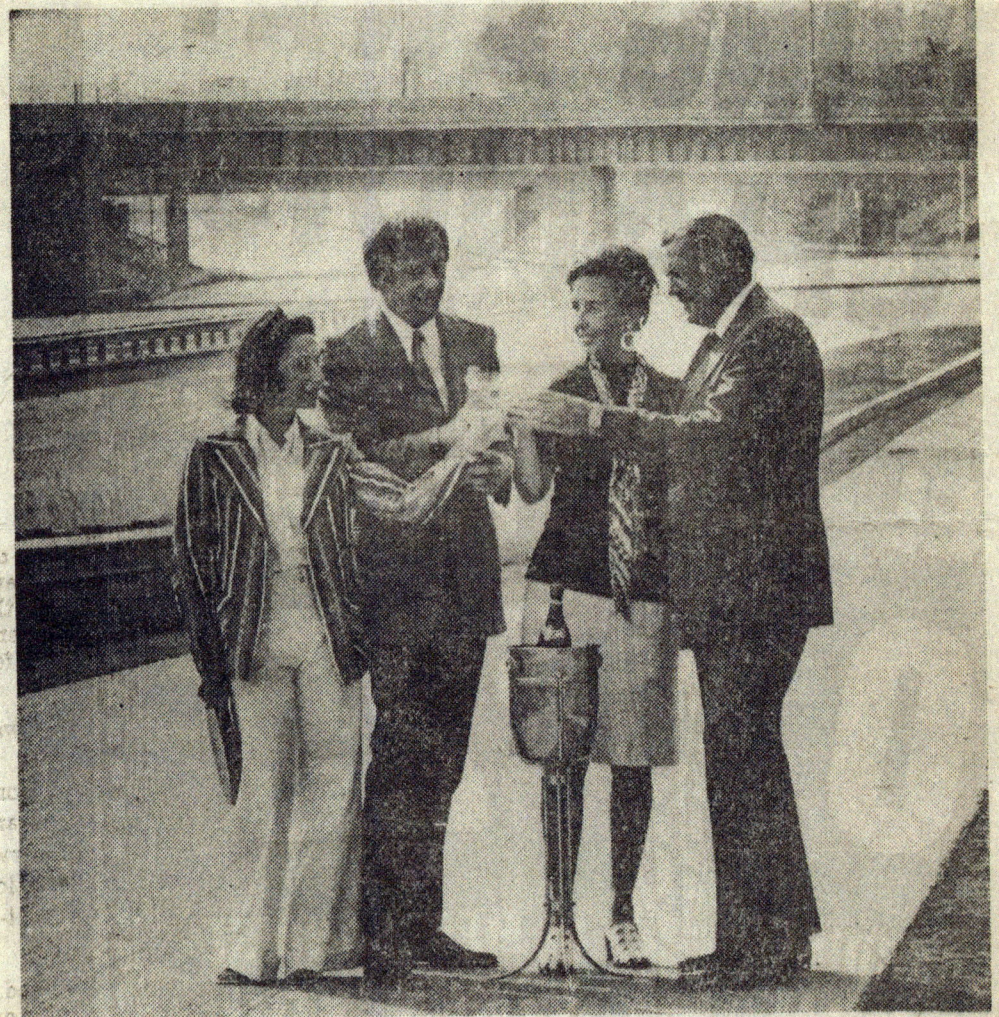

ON THE ROAD TO LAKEWOOD LITTLE THEATRE'S premiere party Sept. 15, 400 guests will sip champagne on the unopened stretch of Interstate 90 in Lakewood. General chairmen Mr. and Mrs. Robert Curry (left), who suggested the site, are working with LLT director and Mrs. Karl Mackey. Champagne will be poured at 6:30 p.m., followed by the show, "The Roar of the Greasepaint and the Smell of the Crowd," at 8 p.m. and dancing and a midnight brunch at Wagner's Country Inn.
(Press photo by Frank Reed)

1973 – The Cleveland Press

By 1972, Lakewood Little Theatre had gained control of about two acres of land fronting a city block on a commercial artery. Board member Ross Ellis took on the role of property manager, working to acquire homes along Wayne and Rockway Avenues to make way for the new addition - the West Shore's first cultural arts center – a $2,000,000 complex embracing all of the arts under one roof.

April 1974 – Campaign press conference at Cleveland Yacht Club

Except for a small Patrons' Fund and a $5,000 grant from the Gund Foundation to install new seats and remodel the auditorium in 1969, the LLT had never before 1974 gone to the public, corporations and foundations for support.

A $600,000 contribution from Mr. Beck - $300,000 of which was to be matched by general public support – was a challenge to the West Shore community. Indeed it was a challenge to the community and also to the organization, since having prided themselves on "never asking anyone for anything," LLT was setting out to request support from the public for the first time in its history. Having established no culture of philanthropy over the previous decades, the organization had no infrastructure (volunteer or staff) in place to conduct a capital campaign and no annual contributors to call upon to start it off.

Mr. Beck was introduced to the media at the Cleveland Yacht Club in April 1974, and the campaign kick-off was held in September 1974 at Westwood Country Club, with Hugh Dawson as general chair of fundraising. Jess Bell of Bonne Bell Cosmetics was chairman of special gifts. Their ambitious goal was to raise $1,500,000 dollars.

Howard Egert recalled (1994 interview), *"It was interesting the way Hugh Dawson would raise money. He raised money in Westwood Country Club locker room frequently. He'd go up to some man and say, 'Give me a thousand dollars.' He'd say, 'What for?' Hugh would say, 'Don't ask questions, just give me a thousand dollars for Beck Center.' And that was it!"*

April 1974 – Campaign press conference at Cleveland Yacht Club

The fundraising effort which enlisted the support of 1700 individuals, corporations and foundations ultimately netted over $1,200,000, including grants from Eaton Corporation, National City Bank, Bonne Bell, George Gund Foundation, John C. Wasmer Foundation (Lake Erie Screw Corp), First Federal Lakewood, and Ohio Arts Council.

Coming attraction: the Lakewood Big Theater

July 1974 Cleveland Press

In a letter from project architect Fred Toguchi to Ken Beck on July 31, 1974, Mr. Toguchi addressed Mr. Beck's request for an apartment on the second or third floor of the Lakewood Little Theatre building. Mr. Toguchi advised against living there. He explained his vision that the existing facilities and new construction be unified architecturally, in order to create a total image for the Center. After much study, he concluded that *"the existing second floor must be virtually devoid of windows, especially large windows, in order to become unified with the new construction of the museum and the auditorium which generally require very little exterior fenestration. In order to maintain unity, we are recommending that little, if any, windows be placed on the second floor of the existing building, particularly on the façade that faces Detroit Avenue."*

July 31, 1974

Mr. Kenneth C. Beck
Kenneth C. Beck Center
  for the Cultural Arts
Lakewood Little Theater
17823 Detroit Avenue
Lakewood, Ohio 44107

Dear Mr. Beck:

I thank you for your letter of July 16, 1974. Your request for the consideration of an apartment on the second or the third floor of the existing building is certainly possible. However, I do want to point out some consideration in regard to the overall development. First of all, an apartment on the third floor would be quite difficult to accomplish, unless you are willing to consider smaller bedroom and living room sizes, inasmuch as expansion of that suite is economically impractical. On the second floor there are places where apartments accommodating the size that you wish is possible and practical. It is with some concern, however, that I make the following qualification. It is, I believe, important in the minds of all of us that in the development of the Kenneth C. Beck Center for the Cultural Arts that the existing facilities and the new construction be unified architecturally. This objective is most important in terms of creating a total image for the Center. That image can be impaired greatly by the manner in which the existing buildings are remodeled. We have found after much study that the existing second floor must be virtually devoid of windows, especially large windows, in order to become unified with the new construction of the museum and the auditorium which generally require very little exterior fenestration. In order to maintain unity, we are recommending that little, if any, windows be placed on the second floor of the existing building, particularly on the facade that faces Detroit Avenue. I ask that you think about some of these architectural consequences of an apartment and ask that you give this matter your deep consideration. I thank you for your interest and expect to see you soon.

Sincerely yours,

FRED TOGUCHI ASSOCIATES, ARCHITECTS

Fred S. Toguchi

FST/me

July 31, 1974 – Letter from Fred Toguchi to Ken Beck

Mr. Toguchi was advising Mr. Beck against living in a building where all the windows were covered. Curiously, no thought was apparently given to the use of a space that appeared so forbidding and hidden to the public. This architectural statement would have an enormous impact on the culture of the institution from that time on.

1977 – The Maheu Building "with very little exterior fenestration" – photo credit Bill Plotz

In a 1994 interview with Dr. Joseph Albrecht (Board President 1980-1990) by Helen Grabner, Dr. Albrecht recalled regarding the new Beck Center, *"The basic problem was moving from being just a theatre into being a cultural center. In other words, there were many new things to be done and of course the first part of the time, the new building was not there… Many people don't realize how fortunate they were that over a period of years that previous Boards of Trustees had seen that it was important to put whatever they could, moneywise, into property around there so that all this property was available…In other words, they were foresighted… It was just a good experience…"*

1974 – "The Garage" with the Armory visible in the background to the right – photo credit Bill Plotz

Photo credit unknown – 1950s – when "The Garage" was a Convertible Top Shop – the annex building is visible in the background

Date unknown – "The Little Gas Station" – photo credit Bill Plotz

The construction site, prior to groundbreaking; the parcel east of the building purchased by LLT in 1963 for $100,000, once held a laundromat, garage, and used car lot, as well as adjacent properties with single- and two-family dwellings. Photo credit Beck Center.

Ground was broken in December 1975, and the Center opened 9 months and 3 weeks later as The Lakewood Little Theatre/Beck Center for the Cultural Arts.

The construction site of the new Beck Center looking northwest from Rockway Avenue
Photo credit Beck Center

Construction site looking south with the Armory in the background 1975
Photo credit Beck Center

The Annex building on the corner of Rockway and Detroit Avenues 1975
Photo credit Beck Center

HIS OWN LOUNGE - Architect Fred Toguchi (left) shows Lakewood businessman William R. Daniels the lounge that will be named after him in honor of his $35,-000 donation to the Kenneth C. Beck Center for the Cultural Arts. Daniels is a funeral director.

(Press photo by Van Dillard)

Arts center to carry donors' names

The Lakewood Little Theater is selling immortality.

For a $250,000 donation the main theater in the Kenneth C. Beck Center for the Cultural Arts will be named in honor of the donor.

For $50,000 builders will name the lecture hall-studio theater for the contributor—and for just $5000 you may have adult education office carry your name.

The donations for name tags are being used to help finance the $2 million theater project at 17823 Detroit Ave., Lakewood. When completed the new home of the Lakewood Little Theater will occupy the entire block.

It's called the Beck Center for Kenneth C. Beck, an 80-year-old retired Lakewood businessman who will have donated a total of $600,000 by the time the buildings are finished.

Some of the areas still available for naming are the galleria at $50,000; the rehearsal room at $20,000; creative music room, ceramics room and studio lobby at $10,-000 each or the main theater light control area for $5000.

More information is available by calling 228-6050.

June 10, 1975 – Cleveland Press

SUNDAY PLAIN DEALER
CLEVELAND, JUNE 29, 1975

Metro

☐Editorials ☐Letters ☐News ☐Features

Construction starts in fall on Beck theater complex

By Pauline Thoma

The spotlight will shine upon the Lakewood Little Theater this fall when construction of a dream begins.

That dream will be the Kenneth C. Beck Center for the Cultural Arts, a $2 million entertainment complex that will cover a city block.

Beck, its chief benefactor, is a retired Lakewood businessman and artist who gave the theater $300,000 in April 1974. He promised a similar amount to match money raised in a public campaign.

The center will be built along the south side of Detroit Ave. from Wayne Ave. to Rockway Ave. at the west end of the city. The present theater at 17823 Detroit will become a restaurant.

The complex will include a 500-seat new theater, a Galleria for display of arts and crafts, children's and teen-age theaters, a 150-seat lecture hall-studio theater, art classrooms, the restaurant and garden courtyard, specialty shops and a museum.

The building fund campaign, directed by Walter S. Weismann Jr., began last September with a goal of $600,000.

Weismann and 500 volunteer workers have collected $400,000 in contributions and pledges thus far. Their success in raising the remaining $200,000 will determine the date of the fall groundbreaking.

A zoning change for the expansion and a variance will be sought Tuesday at a planning commission public hearing by Karl A. Mackey, theater managing director; Fred Toguchi, the architect, and F. Ross Ellis, president of the LLT Fine Arts Foundation.

The theater and its properties along Detroit Ave. are in a retail district. The center will extend south into residential districts on both side streets about 125 feet to encompass six houses the theater has purchased. Permission to extend the retail zoning is needed.

The commission will also be asked to permit the center to build only eight feet from the sidewalks. At present, the limit is 20 feet on Wayne and 15 on Rockway.

Lakewood Planning Director Eric S. Lane foresees no problem in granting the requests.

"I'm sure the city favors this; it's a boon to Lakewood. I'm sure the city favors to have this art center here. The theater has been here a long time, everybody supports it, they need more room and will get it," Lane said.

He also noted that the theater will provide off-street parking.

The City Council has already considered the change in the building line map and an amendment to the zoning code. Two more readings of the changes are needed. Lane said if the changes are approved it would be possible for building permits to be issued by mid-September.

The Ohio Legislature and Gov. James A. Rhodes have already approved the theater's 9,200-square-foot land swap with the Ohio National Guard, which has an armory behind the theater. This will enable consolidation of parking lots for the theater and the National Guard.

Theater trustees, the foundation and volunteers began buying other properties in the theater block 17 years ago. That foresight is paying off now in the new plans for their 2 1/3-acre site.

Among the most successful community theaters in Ohio, LLT has a history of being self-sustaining since its inception 45 years ago.

It began in 1930 as the Guild of the Masques and changed to its present name three years later. It has been providing entertainment ever since in its home, the former Lucier Theater. About 50,000 comedy and drama buffs attend performances there every season, a figure expected to increase when the new facilities open.

The courtyard that will be in the Beck Center.

How buildings in the cultural complex will be used. The second floor of the present theater will contain administrative and rental offices and the second floor of the Galleria will have classrooms and meeting space.

Construction on the main building – December 1975; photo credit Beck Center

December, 1975

The Lakewood Little Theatre building – December 1975 – Photo credit Beck Center

Front entrance 1976 – photo credit Beck Center

1976 – construction site looking west – photo credit Beck Center

1976 – Photo credit Bill Plotz

Front entrance to main building – 1976; photo credit Beck Center

1976 – photo credit Beck Center

Cleveland architect Fred Toguchi designed the plans for the complex which included a dance studio and art classrooms. Karl Mackey had to fight with the utility companies to install gas heating instead of the prohibitively expensive electric. And sudden increases in construction costs made other modifications necessary. "We were the first theatre in Greater Cleveland to have a state of the art computerized light board," says Lighting Engineer, Andrew Kosiorek.

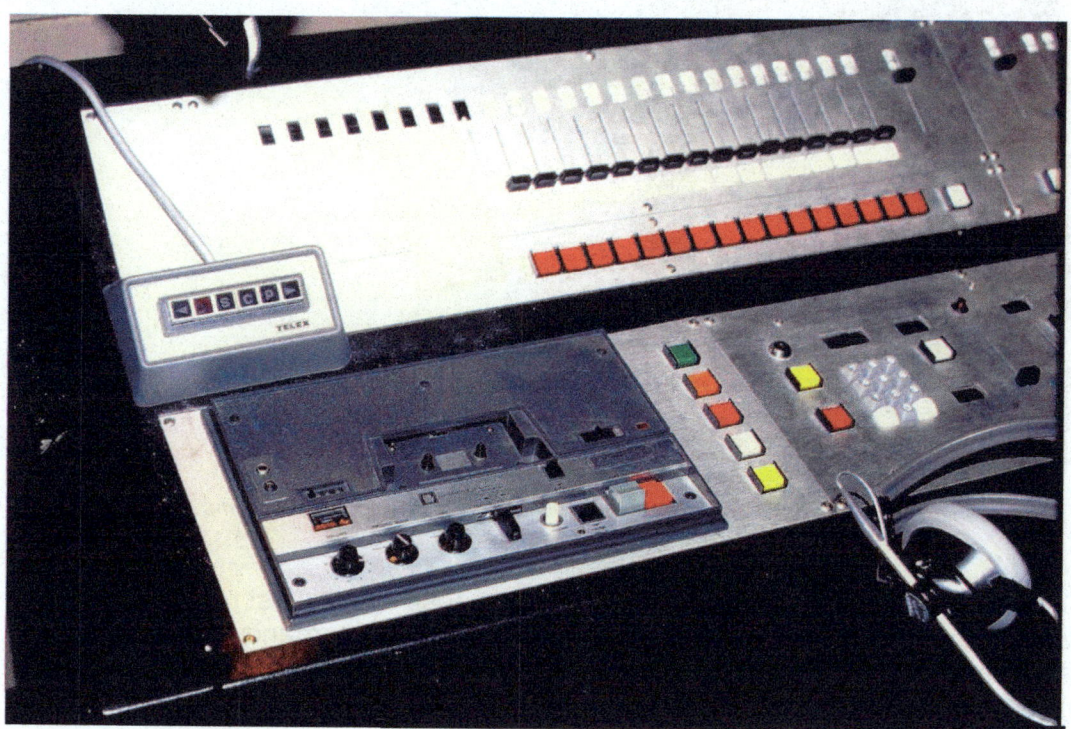

September 1976 – gala opening of Beck Center, Architect Fred and Mrs. Toguchi; photo credit Beck Center

September 1976 – gala opening of Beck Center, Jan and Howard Egert, John and Peggy McFerrin; photo credit Beck Center

The Kenneth C. Beck Center for the Cultural Arts formally opened with its first production, *Mary, Queen of Scots* on October 22, 1976, and the business address of the organization became 17801 Detroit Avenue. In an interview with Bob Curry, he said "*Mary, Queen of Scots was the opening play by Maxwell Anderson, starring Lee Mackey and Nancy Slovenkay. A beautiful production. Really gorgeous. But the opening night was two nights actually. We had a Friday and a Saturday night, but we had the same parties because it was such a demand to come in and see the new buildings"*

1976 – *Mary Queen of Scots* - First Production of Beck Center
Photo credit Beck Center

Critic at Large By Peter Bellamy

Beck Center opens tonight

The birth pangs of a $2-million cultural arts center and theater complex are long and fearful, but they are about to run their course in Lakewood.

They will cease after 28 years tonight when the curtain rises at the new Lakewood Little Theater and the Kenneth C. Beck Center for the Cultural Arts, that covers a city block at 17801 Detroit Ave., in the suburb. It is the first cultural center ever built in the western suburbs.

The elegant, 500-seat theater, with its 42-by-20-foot proscenium frame, arch stage, $62,000 computerized light board and lighting system, accoustical wood walls, ramps for the handicapped, spacious lounge and Galleria for arts and crafts display, are only part of the center.

In addition to the new theater, the center has a second-floor skylight studio with 3,500 square feet of space, which may be divided into three rooms for classes, luncheons, conferences, club meetings and bridge games. It also has a service kitchen for catered meals.

Architect Fred Toguchi has given both the new and old parts of the center a light, airy, cheerful and verdant atmosphere.

Exposed heating, air-conditioning and utility pipes are painted in gay pastels. The structure has many picture windows and there are two gardens in the to be landscaped Harmonic Grid area which faces Detroit Ave.

One of the gardens, a project of the LLT's Women's Board, is in the museum at the eastern end of the Galleria. The other, located in a courtyard enclosed by the new and old buildings, may be seen from the Galleria's glass enclosed esplanade at its western end.

On view tonight at the Galleria's museum will be Floyd Chaney's portrait of Beck, the wealthy, retired Lakewood businessman who gave $600,000 to the center bearing his name, a Cleveland Institute of Art faculty show and a Cleveland Museum of Art modular display.

The Harmonic Grid XLIV, which faces Detroit Ave. adjacent to the theater entrance, was designed by David Davis, and is the 44th in a series of harmonic grids designed by him.

It will feature a metal sculpture designed to denote the infinity of creative art, standing in a grove of trees.

From a theater buff's standpoint, the most fascinating aspect of the theater is its trapdoor system, which may be unique in theater annals.

Its kinship with water relates to that of the famed Paris Opera House, which is connected with the labyrinthine Paris sewers.

Originally, the plans called for the construction of a 3,200 square foot basement underneath the stage of the new theater.

Alas, as Robert Burns once said, "The best laid plans o' mice and men go aft agley."

"We discovered that the land under the stage was atop a prehistoric lake — dubbed Lake Warren — a beach and shale," said Karl Mackey, managing director. "It would have cost us more than $150,000 to drain the water to make the basement possible.

"To save the $150,000 in the face of mounting costs, we decided to eliminate the basement

"We found the only place for the trapdoors was in a vertical line down the center of the stage. The traps are three feet wide, six and a half feet deep and total 40 feet in length in a straight line.

"If we put them in any other place under the stage we would have encountered drainage problems."

The original Lakewood Little Theater, top, gets a face-lifting to match the adjoining new Beck Center, below. The building was designed to preserve the bicentennial maple tree on the right.

It is perhaps significant to note that the Cleveland Institute of Art for the first time in its history will offer outside of its own building credit courses in art at the Beck Center.

The brick facing of the old building has been sandblasted to match as perfectly as possible the brick facing of the new building. The southeast corner of the new building was built so as to preserve a bicentennial maple tree 40 inches in circumference at the trunk.

The center will have off-street parking for 200 cars with more to come in January with the razing of three store fronts on the property.

From the spectator standpoint it is good to know that the last row of seats is only 54 feet from the stage.

There is no orchestra pit. Orchestras will play backstage, which should make it easier to hear the lyrics of songs.

Aside from the $600,000 donated by Beck, the center was made possible by $643,000 raised by the LLT Fine Arts Foundation, $300,000 realized by LLT's borrowing power, a $100,000 grant from the Cleveland Foundation and other donations.

The christening of the center and theater will be celebrated tonight and tomorrow night with presentation of Maxwell Anderson's drama, "Mary of Scotland," featuring Nancy DeCapua, Lee Mackey, James Binns, Nick Brobeila, William Beck, Bob Cochrane and Bob Corns.

On both evenings there will be cocktails, dinner and dancing at the center. Formal dedication of the building will be on Nov. 1. Both Beck and Mackey, the co-fathers, will be present.

Walter S. Weismann Jr., who headed the LLT's fund raising effort without pay, could also pass out cigars.

Forgotten will be past labors of obtaining the land, starting in 1956, the struggle to raise the money, the securing of zoning easements from Lakewood City Council and the approval of a land swap with the National Guard by Gov. James A. Rhodes and the state legislature.

Karl Mackey, managing director of the old and new Lakewood Little Theater, takes a call in the new Beck Center.

The Skylight Studio (3,400sqft), on the 2nd floor of the main building, overlooked an enclosed courtyard. This was intended to be a multi-purpose space for dinner before theater performances, for weddings and receptions for up to 200 people, and public meetings. Soon after, classrooms were built into the space in order to accommodate the growing education program.

Inner courtyard garden – photo credit Beck Center

The Beck Center Museum was one of the outstanding exhibit spaces in the Greater Cleveland area, with 3400sqft of space consisting of two galleries, and an indoor garden as the focal point separating the two. The Museum offered eight or nine exhibits each year, timed with the theater schedule to take advantage of the traffic generated by the LLT performances. Regularly scheduled exhibitions were free and open to the public.

1976 Gallery – photo credit Beck Center

Beck Center: . . . "chocolate brown wall helps create a warm, inviting entrance to the center."

Among the "little surprises:" art work and live plantings as one walks through the center.

Beck Center—a handsome patch on Detroit Ave.

By James M. Wood

If buildings are the fabric with which a city is built, architects Fred Toguchi and Associates have put a handsome patch on Detroit Ave.

The design of the Kenneth C. Beck Center for the Cultural Arts in Lakewood courageously reaches out with a bag full of urban design tricks to use homes, stores, sidewalks, street, trees, grass and the center itself to build a new framework for a blighted thoroughfare.

Architects and planners like the "fabric" metaphor. It helps them explain their attempts to take individual buildings and their relationships to neighboring structures and create diverse spaces for people to use in the city.

Unfortunately, the importance of fabric has not always been recognized.

The leveling of all the buildings in Erieview dissolved the fabric. Bleak plazas in desolate urban renewal projects taught us a lesson. It's not just the plaza that counts; what surrounds it is important, too. Would you rather watch skaters at Rockefeller Center or in front of Erieview?

Detroit Avenue has fabric, but it's a shoddy piece of goods.

Anyone interested in how urban design can make a city more humane should drive Detroit Ave. toward the Beck. It's in the 17800 block. From east or west the dreary streetscape is equally repulsive. From the barbed-wire-topped fence surrounding the Club Products Co. parking lot to the macabre welcome offered by the manicured front lawns of the funeral homes, it's not an attractive place.

Even the spurt of highrises that occurs around St. Charles Street doesn't relieve the monotony of blocks and blocks of structures built right up to the sidewalk. Add the garish signs, unsightly overhead wires, and a general shabbiness and you have a picture of Detroit. Every American city has similar streets.

Toguchi offers us an alternative at the Beck. Suddenly a void appears in the row of buildings. From the east there is a hint of something special with the prominent wood-paneled exterior of the old apartment building that houses the Beck Center and Lakewood Little Theater offices.

From the west a building's simple brick endwall, painted a rich chocolate brown, quietly says (if you will pardon just this once the attribution of speech to an inanimate object) "Look here, I've got a surprise for you."

The surprise is the Center: located about 50 feet from the sidewalk atop a grassy knoll and slightly out of parallel with Detroit. The building's siting draws your attention to its presence and establishes its identity as a special place.

The humble brown brick, simple bronze aluminum details, and gray-white skylights are an understated backdrop to a bright orange and black sculpture by David Davis: another interesting interplay between solids and voids.

Alternative to urban monotony is offered in Lakewood—by design

Toguchi's site plan leaves spacious green areas along the eastern sidewalk, extending the line of neighborhood lawns. Parking is arranged around the building. Nowhere are cars allowed to dominate the landscape.

A fine old silver maple was saved just a few feet from the east end of the structure. On the west side, the new center meets the old Lakewood Little Theater building at the "ell" formed by the old auditorium and storefront wings. It's where they used to pile the trash.

Now the area is a gracefully landscaped outdoor courtyard, enclosed by brick walls of both old and new buildings, and a handsome glass and wood arcade, just one of the surprises that Toguchi and his associates provide inside the building.

The stark white interior walls are an understated background to the color and movement of people. Toguchi has placed openings in walls that provide unusual vantage points for people to watch each other.

"We tried to build in little surprises as a person walks through the center. An arts building should not be a monotonous experience. It should embody the expectations people have for the artistic experience," Toguchi said.

The design has been meticulously followed by the general contractor Aulcar Construction. The total building cost $1.5 million, and was constructed for $35 a square foot; not bad for a quality building in the highly inflationary construction industry.

There is one unsettling piece of news. The small commercial structure at the east end of the site on Detroit — the one with the chocolate brown wall — may have to be demolished early next year. Originally, the building was to house a restaurant. The cost of remodeling and the lack of on-site parking meant those plans had to be abandoned.

Karl Mackey, executive director for the Center, believes the location of the building is "aesthetically" wrong.

"Our new center shouldn't be behind this old structure," he said. "I would like to replace it with some more parking and some landscaping."

The building's no jewel, that's for sure; but a line of cars wouldn't be any better. And that modest chocolate brown wall helps create a warm, inviting entrance to the center. With the wall gone, the plaza enclosure will evaporate.

It won't be like Erieview, but it won't be as nice as it is now.

When the Center board votes in January about what to do with the building, let's hope they find a way to refurbish the old structure or build a new one.

They have done such good work already it would be shame for that elegant patch to unravel.

Ken Beck was on site almost daily while the addition was being built and attended the opening of the 1977-1978 season, before he died in 1977. Karl Mackey was quoted as saying "He did see the place in existence for a full year…and there are those who say this whole project prolonged his life." Mr. Beck said to Lynda Sackett shortly before he died, "I never dreamed I could be this happy!"

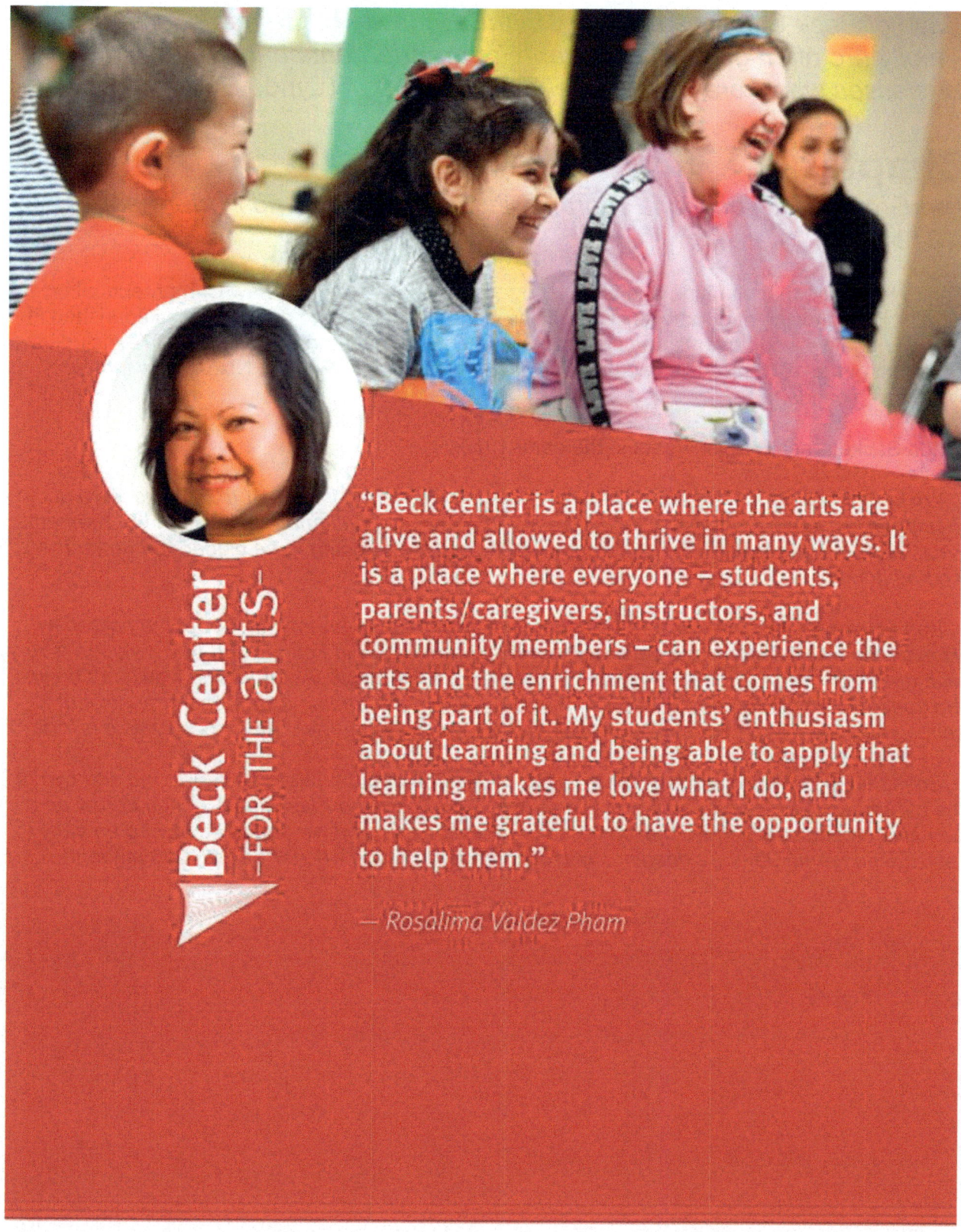

Beck Center
—FOR THE arts—

"Beck Center is a place where the arts are alive and allowed to thrive in many ways. It is a place where everyone – students, parents/caregivers, instructors, and community members – can experience the arts and the enrichment that comes from being part of it. My students' enthusiasm about learning and being able to apply that learning makes me love what I do, and makes me grateful to have the opportunity to help them."

— Rosalima Valdez Pham

"Love of Beck Center is exhibited in the longevity of the arts education staff. Faculty are often greeted by parents or grandparents bringing their children for classes who were once students themselves." (Lynda Sackett)

Chapter 8:

The Growth of Education Programming, Exhibitions, and Performances – (1973-1999)

During the years that planning and fundraising were underway for the new Center, education classes kept growing stronger. As in past years, arts education and performances flourished in spite of negative world events and societal challenges. Indeed, major events in 1974 include the aftermath of the 1973 oil crisis and the resignation of President Richard Nixon following the Watergate scandal.

Lynda Sackett recalls those years in the early 1970s:

...While I was with the Children's Theatre, Jan kept whispering in my ear that things were going to happen. Things were really going to break. There was a gentleman by the name of Kenneth Beck, and he was really a very generous person, and it was going to be bigger and better than we had hoped...

...Karl Mackey invited several people to come to a meeting to brainstorm about the potential uses for the Beck Center, and potential sources of funding. And I suggested that we open a very high quality dancing school, with professional, performing artists. And that this would not be just the general commercial kind of school. This would be more leading toward the professional school, and it would attract adults...I outlined the Dance Department then, exactly as it is today.

...So in the fall, Wilma Salisbury came to Beck Center and did a photo story with me and two of the other teachers, and gave us one full page in The Cleveland Plain Dealer. Then I drew up a beautiful brochure, which we mailed out to our audition list. And we ended up having an early registration for our January opening. We registered early, and we started with 200 students...

Ready to welcome dance students to the new Beck Center in Lakewood are (from left) dance department director Lynda Sackett, modern dance instructor Grayce Dolesh and ballet teacher Nina Packard Long.

Lynda Sackett, Grayce Dolesh, Nina Long

Ms. Sackett founded the Dance Department in 1976 with sequential courses in ballet, jazz, modern and tap - for children and adults of all ages and abilities - in one dance studio. (The first dance studio was in the rear of the auditorium of the LLT, with a "sleepered" floor installed over the sloped theater floor and wooden sprung floor over that. This still exists as of 2022.)

A performance workshop company for serious dance students leading to advanced studies and/or professional careers was also offered along with early childhood dance readiness classes for preschool age children. In later years, hip-hop, pilates, and somatic exercise classes (i.e., "Body Beautiful") were added. Having had considerable experience in commercial dance studios, Ms. Sackett wanted to avoid spending money on splashy costumes and devoting months of rehearsals to a few pieces, she was adamant about focusing on the students and stressing serious dance education.

The program flourished along with a dire need for more space. Master classes with nationally recognized dance artists, dance concerts, and a dance company (Dance Theatre Workshop) were established, first under Diane Ryan and continued under Melanie Szucs[6], to the writing of this book. Dance Theatre Workshop participated annually in Northeast Ohio Dance Festivals.

Grayce Dolesh a.k.a. Stormy, was a long time dance teacher at the Beck Center. She began teaching her S.M.I.L.E. Classes[7] with the opening of the Beck Center Dance Department. These classes were for preschoolers with emphasis on coordination and movement concepts helpful in school for academic learning. She cared deeply about her students, and was especially helpful when assisting children with disabilities. She received the Educator of the Year Award from the Council for Exceptional Children. She was a Certified Teacher for Adventures in Movement for the Handicapped. She was Movement Therapist for the Independence Schools. As a former modern dancer, she was an active member of Cleveland Modern Dance Association West (DanceCleveland).

In 1976, the Board of Trustees was expanded from 15 to 24 members, recognizing the new center's need for versatile expertise. In 1980, six additional trustee positions were created. This 30-member Board united the rich heritage of the LLT with the strong guidance necessary for the growth and direction of Beck Center.

Also by 1976, the Children's/Teen Theatre offered basic training in theater and stage techniques to hundreds of students. The school was a member of the American Theatre Association of Kennedy Center.

---

[6] See APPENDIX A

[7] S.M.I.L.E.: Sensory Motor Integrated Learning Experiences

October 22, 1976 - Adventures of Young Ben Franklin - (L to R) John Thompson, Tom Humphrey, Ernest Green
Photo credit Humbert Studios

1976-77 Awards Night – (L-R) Bernice Bolek, Bruce Wacker, Nancy DeCapua, Earl Heiden
Photo credit Beck Center

Music Presentations

Between 180 and 200 performances were offered each year, including theater productions and special events. Led by Dorothy Myers (a former Lakewood Little Theatre actress), the Spotlight Series was created, featuring musical concerts and recitals by established professional performing arts groups, including the Alvin Ailey Repertory Dance Ensemble, jazz pianist Paul Posnak, folk singer Odetta, the noted Carlos Montoya, Anna Russell, Les Ballets Jazz de Montreal and over 50 others. An advertising program funded by The Standard Oil Company of Ohio helped the Center reach a larger potential audience. Russ Rissman, technical director for all productions worked with Karl Mackey and Lynda Sackett on the Spotlight Series.

In a 1994 interview, Dorothy Myers shared her memories about her work during the late 1970s as Director of the Spotlight Series:

"I felt that since we were a Cultural Arts Center that we absolutely needed music. There was no music at that time in the Beck Center. And so, I had a meeting with Karl Mackey and he said 'Well, if you want to do it, I just assume it's as a volunteer'…My idea was to use the wealth of musical talent in this city, and to give them a venue through which they could use their talents. We have the Cleveland Opera, the Cleveland Orchestra, also the Cleveland Institute of Music. It was my idea to start a music program with local talent of the highest quality of excellence. But I didn't have any money for it, so I had to beg, borrow and steal for the performers. And many of them were willing to perform free…The first concert was my brother from Detroit who was a very well-known tenor…Then I called David Bamberger and asked him if he would like to get a group of singers from the Cleveland Opera together and do a program called 'Opera Just For Fun.' We did that, and I don't think they got any pay for that either…And then one concert – I think the third concert – was Ronnie Horowitz. He was Professor of Music at the Cleveland Institute of Music. Outstanding violinist. To give you an idea, he gave the concert here – I think it was on a Tuesday night – and the next morning he flew to do a concert at Carnegie Hall in New York City…It was really difficult starting music programming in a house that had not done music programming before. In fact, I'm not even sure if, at that time, they were playing musicals…

…The thought came to me of how I would like to do a chamber production of Handel's "Messiah." I thought 'What can I do?' I can go to the Cleveland Opera, and I can call Robert Paige (whom I had never met) and I can present a budget to him and see if he would be willing to put together a group from the Cleveland Opera to do a chamber production of 'Messiah.'…He was so ecstatic about the idea – we just hit it off like magic… and he said 'You get the funding, and I'll do it for free.' Well, that really was the embryonic stage or the beginning of the eventual 'Robert Paige Singers'."

The noted Robert Paige Singers eventually used Beck Center as "home" for rehearsals and performances for many years.

Since at least 1995 and throughout the following decades, Beck Center has enjoyed the generous support of the Kulas Foundation whose primary purpose is to fund music and music education in the Greater Cleveland area.

Richard Farmer, performing artist, Spotlight Series, wrote "There is a feeling of excitement, almost familial attachment and involvement in the arts that is at once intangible and utterly infectious."

Mini art course offered at Beck

The Cleveland Museum of Art will offer a free four-part mini course starting at 1:30 p.m. Wednesday in Beck Center.

To introduce the major traveling exhibition of "The Realist Tradition: French Painting and Drawing 1830-1900," is the reason the course is being offered. The special exhibit will be at the museum from Nov. 12 through Jan. 18.

The first three sessions are slide-lectures at Beck in Lakewood and the fourth lecture will be presented at the art museum plus a guided tour of the exhibition.

Rocky River Public Library will host the mini-course at 7:30 p.m. on the same days scheduled for Beck, Oct. 29, Nov. 5 and 12.

To register, participants must obtain forms from Beck or the River library. Registrations will be accepted through the first session at each location

Telephone registrations will not be accepted. But, for additional information on the courses, call Ellen Breitman at 421-7340, ext. 404.

SPOTLIGHT STAR — Bay Village resident, pianist, teacher Marianne Mastics will be presented in concert as the first performance in the Spotlight Series at Beck Center. Ms. Mastics will feature the works of Chopin and Gershwin at 3 p.m. Sunday. Tickets are $6 a person and reservations may be made by calling the Beck box office at 521-2540.

October 23, 1980 – Sun Herald

Visual Arts Exhibitions and Beck Center Art

In a 1994 interview with Director of Art Jayne Wells by Nick Brodella, Ms. Wells recalled how she became Art Director, following years of running props, painting sets, and hemming curtains:

"Karl Mackey would come backstage and before, or when I had time, I would be working on my macramé. Karl was interested in that, and I think he knew I was doing clay at the time, and that I had studied Fine Arts. I guess it was just natural for him to call on me and ask, 'Would you like to be the Art Director in 1975?' We had not opened here yet, but he wanted me to get ready to be the Art Director…I had started with mini-classes over in the gas station – when we had the little gas station. Art Kuhl was a friend of Russ Rissman, and Art had said, 'Let's start clay.' He really started everything because he had a potter's wheel and he had a kiln. Karl let him have the gas station, I guess, and then he moved over to the electric shop. Then I was teaching in the gas station, and I taught clay in the electric place… It was the old electric shop… But when we moved into the Beck Center, then they took the corner here to make it into a pottery shop for me…Karl was already a friend of someone from the Art Institute, and he wanted to have classes here with the Art Institute. I had to get those all attended to before we opened, because Karl wanted the classes to be taught by teachers of the Art Institute background. Like Merlin Van Glahn, everybody had a degree, or Masters, or Doctorate. Merlin Van Glahn was in calligraphy, and I needed to keep my classes on the same par as the Art Institute. The Art Institute was here, I believe, three years. Richard Treaster, Julian Stanbach, and his wife Barbara Stanbach from the Cleveland Institute of Art also taught here…We had all kinds of classes – we had paper making, clay wheel, clay hand building. We had Chinese brush, which is the backward painting…we decided we should have a juried show once a year. Merlin Van Glahn thought up the name, 'Proscenium.' She said that's what it should be, because it's the opening and broadening of the proscenium arch to include the visual arts… That brought a lot of people here…I guess the Museum was exclusively for the more costly shows, because it could be locked. And it had a garden so it could show more costly paintings or sculptures, or quilts, or

whatever… And the Galleria was for people to come in and buy – to see something that wasn't real expensive, or something maybe they could use."

Each year the number of entries featuring artists and craftsmen for the Center's Juried Art Show titled "Proscenium" continued to increase and grow in stature. The Beck Museum hosted several fine exhibitions presented in cooperation with the Cleveland Museum of Art. National attention was focused on a unique exhibition created for the Center by Board Member Joseph Erdelac entitled "A Clevelander Collects Cleveland Artists – 1894 to 1984," including works from his private collection. A holiday invitational offered works for sale. Joe was forever grateful to Karl Mackey for this opportunity which set him on the new path of becoming a well-known art collector and dealer.

"We had people coming from all over Cuyahoga County for classes. The majority was always west side – Rocky River, Westlake, Bay Village, Lakewood, Fairview – that was about 50%. The other 50% was south side of town and east side. They were coming from all over!" Roslynne Drake, Visual Arts Faculty

In cooperation with Cleveland Institute of Art, Beck Center presented "Art of Car Design" with six full-sized cars on display in the gallery in 1987. Windows in the Daniels Lounge were removed, and the cars were driven into the building from there.

From the Archives of the Cleveland Institute of Art at the Jessica R. Gund Memorial Library

In October, 1976, the first of several sculptures planned for the Beck Center was commissioned by the Board and selected by architect Fred Toguchi. The work was designed by well-known Cleveland sculptor David Davis, and is titled "Harmonic Grid XLIV," the 44th in a series by Davis.

David Davis (1920-2009), "Harmonic Grid XLIV" – lovingly restored in 2008, thanks to Bernice S. Davis
Photo credit Beck Center

Several artists had contacted Beck Center with offers to provide a piece of sculpture for the new building, so the Board extended an invitation to area artists through the New Organization for the Visual Arts (NOVA). Later two additional sculptures were added to the front yard, "Overture" by John Clague and "Flora Bella" by David Deming in November, 2020.

"Overture" – John Clague (1928-2004) – photo credit Beck Center

July 1980 – Sculpture commissioned from Clarence Van Duzer (1920-2009) for Beck Center by the Lakewood Arts Festival
(L to R) Lakewood Mayor Anthony Sinagra, Lucy Sinagra, Artist Clarence Van Duzer; the piece was lovingly restored in 2012 thanks to Kathy Lynn Van Duzer

A building on the corner of Rockway and Detroit Avenues was purchased with the intention of housing the Koch School of Music (later called Riverside Music Academy), dance and choral rooms, plus additional space for commercial property. No information was found on the evolution of that thought process, but in February 1978, the firm Hurd-Gibson-Mikolay, Inc. (HGM, a commercial real estate company) entered into a 20 year lease of a portion of the property with LLT/Beck Center. Beck Center archive records also show that Riverside Academy rented space in the Annex for Music Therapy Classes, from September 1998-1999.

In a Cleveland Press article dated August 30, 1979, Karl Mackey talked about the plans to expand classes, including the addition of music classes and more musical events in the auditorium. To finance that and help pay off a sizeable mortgage, the group had begun seeking additional funds from foundations and government agencies like the Ohio Arts Council. *"It's essential that we now go after a broader base of support in the community,"* he said. He also suggested taking the "little" out of Lakewood Little Theatre but several Board members said they would not support a professional theater, that they believed a community theater was important.

In 1979, Mr. Mackey was honored by Beck Center's Board of Trustees when they named the main theater the Karl A. Mackey Auditorium. The Mackey Theatre name graced every production announcement and publicity of the organization for 40 years, until the Board voted in 2020 to rename it in recognition of Wally and Joyce Senney who made a $1,000,000 philanthropic investment in the organization's future. In January 2022, the Board voted to name the stage of the Senney Theater, the "Mackey Stage," recognizing that as of 2022, Karl Mackey had directed the largest number of productions (173) in the history of the organization. The next largest number of productions directed as of January 2022 is Scott Spence (114), although his number is still rising.

In 1983, through the cooperation of the State of Ohio and the City of Lakewood, Beck Center was able to acquire the 12,000sqft Armory building, located directly behind the main building (54,000sqft). Following renovation, Beck Center had additional space for music and dance classrooms, performances, costume storage, master classes, lectures, and demonstrations, as well as a large kitchen-equipped meeting hall for community dances and meetings.

"...a community theater – that has professional standards – doesn't have to take a back seat to any theater in the country."

From the memorial tribute to Karl A Mackey, October 26, 2002 at Beck Center

In a 1994 interview, Ms. Sackett recalled:
...I wanted the dance program to be more than just a dancing school...We brought in the Alvin Ailey Repertory Company which was a huge, tremendous thing. We had two sold out dance concerts with them...I contacted Bert Holt with Cleveland Public Schools...and she got us – we said we wanted our focus to be to children – and she got us 500 students from the Cleveland School of the Arts who came. When they saw the performance, they screamed bloody murder! It was that exciting! It was that fabulous! And so I began to have an 'in.' Then we did Les Ballets Jazz de Montreal. Another phenomenal company! And again we brought children in. We brought in 'Peanut Butter and Jelly,' and various other groups that involved school children. And each time we did that, I developed more and more access with the schools. Thus it was a logical step for me to become Outreach Director, because I already had input – I already knew many of the educators and what they were looking for. So that is, very briefly, how it happened..."

As a result of this acquisition and grants from the State of Ohio and The Gund Foundation, in 1984 the Board and staff reimagined the space in the main building by adding an 84-seat Studio Theater (later enlarged to 95 seats), and creating a backstage space/"rehearsal hall" next to the Dance Studio. An attempt was made to include sound isolation between the Studio Theater and Dance Studio, but it was never enough to allow dance classes and performances to occur at the same time. Dance and theater continued to be challenged for space, especially on Saturdays.

A second theater had been a part of the Beck Center plan even before the 1976 facility was completed. The Managing Director and the Board of Trustees believed that a smaller theater was extremely important for a number of reasons. There are many people who are interested in the theater but who are not motivated by popular dramatic productions or musicals. Their interest lies in unusual, experimental works more suited to a house seating well under 500. The productions presented each season in the main theater were selected to have broad appeal, the income from which could help to cover the cost of more experimental efforts in the smaller venue.

The first season in the Studio Theater began in December 1984 with "Lizzie Borden in the Late Afternoon." Between the two theaters, Beck Center's season included a back-breaking total of 12 plays and musicals. And, all the while, the youth theater productions were also going strong.

REGISTRATION for LAKEWOOD LITTLE THEATRE SCHOOL
for CHILDREN/TEENS is SATURDAY, FEBRUARY 4, 1984, 10:00
to 12:00 Noon, Beck Center Lobby. All students, former and new,
MUST be registered on or before February 4.
TUITION: $45.00 per semester. Additional students in the same family
receive tuition reduction.
CLASSES begin SATURDAY, FEBRUARY 11, 1984 and through
Saturday, May 5. Classes will NOT be held on the Saturday before
Easter.
CLASSES for students age 7 thru 10 — 9:30 to 11:00 AM.
    students age 11 thru 15 — 11:00 AM to 12:30 PM.
    Teen Theatre ages 16 and older — 11 AM to 12:30 PM.
CURRICULUM: A continuous course composed of major levels of
theatre training which includes: Speech & Communication skills, Script
study; Creative Dramatics/Improvisation, Pantomime; Oral Interpre-
tation/Characterization; Dance/Body Moves/Body Language; Theatre
Music and Audition Techniques. Technical Theatre is offered to older
students.
FACULTY: *Creative Dramatics/Script Study,* Colleen Lanning, Tom McSweeney,
    Nan Ellen Passant, Ted Siller, Dominic Stroffolio, Jr.
    Communication Skills/Oral Interpretation, Rebecca Niemiec, Connie
    Smialek.
    Dance, Colleen Clark, Deborah DeGrange, Deborah Risko.
    Theatre Music/Audition Technique, Jack Kocher, Tamara Beall.
    Teen Theatre/Technical, Tom McSweeney, Robert Lanning.
    Director of LLT School for Children/Teens, Janet Jackson Egert.

Special Thanks to LLT students for "Cinderella":
    Prop Assistants: Paula Rivalsky, Caroline Spisak, Christine Siebert,
        Robbie Killius.
    Light Crew: Wade Gilcher, Bryan Pace, Kevin O'Callaghan, Joey
        Hale.
Stage Crew Cast Members, Additional Thanks to:
    Neil Fowles, John Short, Tom Wilmer, Bob Schafrick, Phillip
    Rendiero, Scott Welty, Mike Parish, Meg Swor, Linda Ostrowski,
    Mike Strauss, Tom Morris, Fred Shoemaker, Andy Kosoriek, Tom
    Vasko, Russ Rissman.
Special appreciation to Educational Theatre Board, parent's support group,
    who volunteer time and effort to LLT School's productions.

Thirty-Fifth Anniversary Season
1983 - 1984

Lakewood Little Theatre School
for Children & Teens
presents

"CINDERELLA"

Music Theatre International
based on the Fairy Tale by Charles Perrault

Director: Tamara Beall
Musical Director: Jack Kocher
Choreographer: Deborah DeGrange

Friday,	January 27, 1984	7:30 PM
Saturday,	January 28, 1984	1:00 PM and 3:30 PM
Sunday,	January 29, 1984	2:00 PM and 4:30 PM
Friday,	February 3, 1984	7:30 PM
Saturday,	February 4, 1984	1:00 PM and 3:30 PM
Sunday,	February 5, 1984	2:00 PM and 4:30 PM

Produced by Jan Egert

Special Arrangement with Music Theatre International

LAKEWOOD LITTLE THEATRE/BECK CENTER
17801 DETROIT AVENUE   **(216) 521-2540**

Box Office Open Monday through Saturday
9:00 AM to 9:00 PM
Sunday 12:00 Noon to 9:00 PM
All Seats Reserved $3.00
Groups of Twenty or More $2.50

With the support of the
Ohio Arts Council

1983-1984 LLT School for Children/Teens Playbill for *Cinderella*

1984 – *Cinderella*; photo credit Humbert Studio

December 9, 1984 – Grand Opening of the Studio Theatre – "Lizzie Borden in the Late Afternoon"
Jim Lipscomb, Dr. Joseph Albrecht; photo credit Beck Center

On June 5, 1986, the Sun Herald announced Karl Mackey's retirement with the following headline: "Curtain falls on Mackey's 32-year run at LLT." The Chamber of Commerce honored him as Lakewood's Citizen of the Year. Mr. Mackey believed strongly in the importance of exposure to the arts and was quoted in the Sun Herald article saying, *"Without it, we're a pretty sorry society. Theater not only entertains, but it informs and sways people, and we need to foster that in every walk of life."*

In a 1994 interview with longtime volunteer, Women's Board member, and Honorary Board Member Marjorie Wiese, she recalled, *"There was a search for the Artistic Director, and that was quite a problem. I mean, to replace Karl Mackey! You know, to bring in a new director after Karl had been Managing Director and Artistic Director for those thirty-two years!"*

The Board hired Fred Sternfeld to be the Artistic Director in April 1986 in anticipation of Karl Mackey's retirement on June 30, 1986. A Cleveland native and graduate of Kent State University, with postgraduate work at Pennsylvania State University, Mr. Sternfeld had been cultural and performing arts director at the Jewish Community Center in Dallas since 1984 and frequently directed in Cleveland area community theaters before that. The Board welcomed Mr. Sternfeld's change in organizational culture, feeling that he would professionalize the theater program. There were very few auditions open to the greater community, which meant the usual cast of west-side favorite actors were left out in favor of a network Mr. Sternfeld knew from his work in eastern suburbs. In an article by Plain Dealer theater critic Marianne Evett on April 26, 1986, Mr. Sternfeld was quoted saying he was especially excited by the new Studio Theater, where he expected to produce "more risky works, where we will not have to worry about the box office."

Also during this time, Cleveland experienced the reopening of the newly renovated Playhouse Square theaters – the Ohio in 1982, the State in 1984, and the city's beloved Palace in 1988.

Audience numbers dropped off, as well as volunteers. The number of volunteers at Beck Center also decreased as the culture began to change from grassroots to professional.

Following a site visit by a program officer of the Ohio Arts Council on December 5, 1986, the report stated:

> "The staff and Board of the Beck Center are trying to expand audience involvement beyond the predominantly white, middle-class community in which the center is located... The audience of about 300 that attended the performance I saw was all white and mostly senior citizens. This should be (and I believe is) of concern to those administering the program. Major marketing efforts are going to have to be made to bring younger adults into the center as well as to expand the audience base to include minority representation.

> Faith Killius, the acting general manager, was thrust into this position only recently upon the retirement of the former general manager." (Karl Mackey) "Both in terms of artistic direction and management, this is a critical transitional time for Beck Center. The former general manager was both artistic director and managing director...not prone to employment of modern methods and strategies in the management, marketing and development of a cultural center.

> The quality and diversity of the art exhibitions in both the museum and the galleria were quite high. The museum was exhibiting a juried show of paintings and sculpture. This show is an annual event and apparently quite popular. There were 725 submissions for the show. Styles ranged from traditional, representational to modern, abstract. I was impressed that the show maintained a high level of artistic integrity with seemingly no compromises for popular taste. The show in the galleria was much more mainstream in content, but still of fairly high artistic quality. Shows change periodically. The Beck Center relies quite heavily on loan exhibitions from the Cleveland Museum of Art.

> The Beck Center suffers from a similar institutional identity as does Karamu House, namely it is known for its parts rather than for its whole. The theater program is the area that most people in the community know of. This is not necessarily bad because the theater program seems to be of high quality. I am quite impressed by the diversity of scripts that are produced – hardly the normal fare for middle-class community theatre. The staff and Board feel a need, however, to communicate that the Beck Center is more than just a theatre and a museum, that it is a multi-purpose cultural and educational resource for the whole community. They feel, and I agree, that until that message is understood, the Beck Center will continue to have problems generating the unearned income necessary to continue and expand their program."

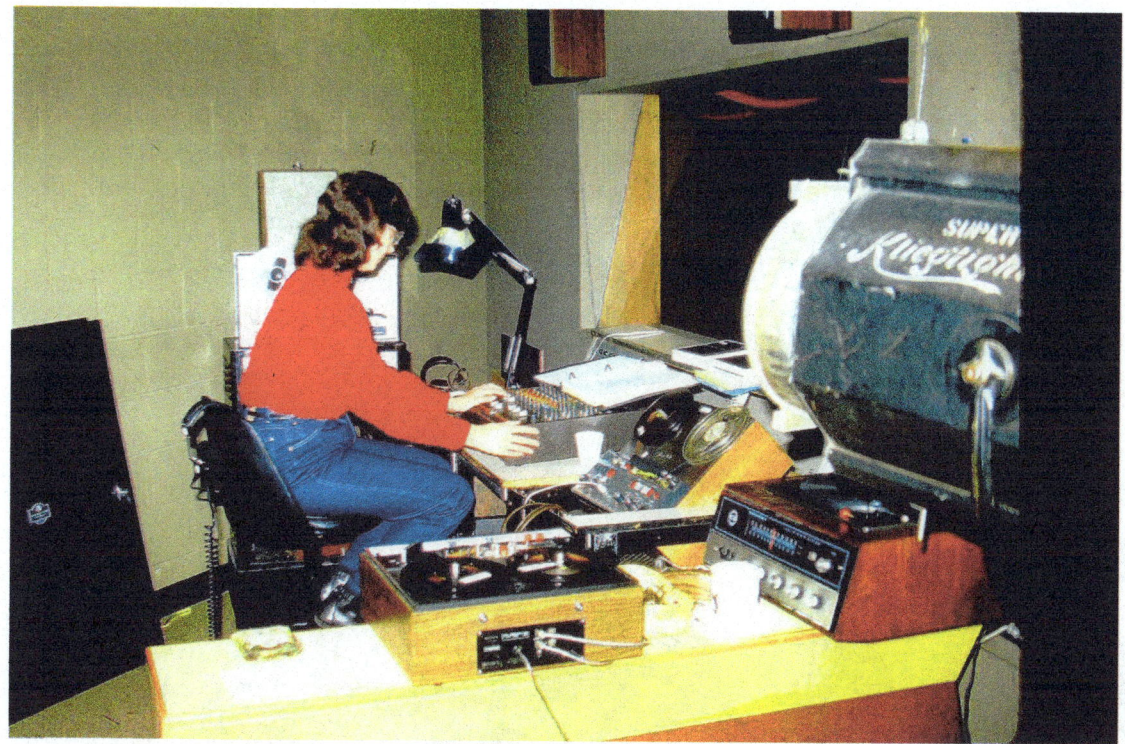

1980s – Sound booth; photo credit Beck Center

The new facility proved to be a mixed blessing. It took the LLT from a small community theater to the major league of cultural arts education. But after the new $3,000,000 facility was completed in 1976, Beck Center was hit with:

- Inflation in wages, materials and services
- High energy costs
- Increased employee costs
- Skyrocketing insurance costs
- Competition from Playhouse Square, Cleveland Play House, and others at University Circle

Between 1982 and 1986, Beck Center had a deficit of $300,000 and substantial debt from the building construction project in spite of:

- Paying minimum wages and eliminating benefits
- Postponing vital maintenance and repairs
- Not having necessary administrative positions filled for director of marketing, manager of operations and director of development
- The donation of time from a large team of volunteers acting as ushers, ticket takers and a variety of other important functions
- An ambitious rental program of valued spaces being used for receptions, club and civic meetings, and even a church

Volunteers were still playing leadership roles within the organization, including the Women's Board and the Drama Production Wing. From the "Drama Production Wing Constitution" – December 1, 1982:

Participation in Drama Production Wing activities shall be expected of every member. Activities shall include the following:

  (a) Reasonable attendance at DPW meetings and special activities, or
  (b) Participation in at least one regular theatre production each season through any one of the following volunteer phases: acting, book-holding, checkroom, costuming, lighting, properties, ushering, clerical, house management, stage management, set construction, sound, set décor, and other scheduled activities which may be undertaken by the Drama Production Wing.

1987 – Dance Class; photo credit Beck Center

The organization was feeling the reality of not having developed a culture of philanthropy over the first decades of its existence. To recover from the financial damage over the previous ten years, Beck Center's Board embarked upon a "60th Anniversary Campaign" in 1986 to raise $3.5M to add administrative staff, eliminate debt from the 1976 construction project, make needed repairs and create an endowment. Funds for the endowment were sought from individuals; corporations were asked for funds for the renovations; foundations were asked to give for employee needs, including additional positions, providing health insurance, and market wages. By March of 1989, pledges and gifts received for the 60th Anniversary Campaign totaled $1,514,000.

The President of the Board at that time was Joseph Albrecht, General Manager Faith Killius, Artistic Director Fred Sternfeld, Peter Metzloff was Campaign Chairman, with Honorary Co-Chairs Richard Celeste, Karl Mackey, Patrick Sweeney, and Anthony Sinagra.

Statistics in 1987

- 200,000 use Beck Center every year[8]
- 250 performances in the Main and Studio Theater
- 600 volunteers, ushers, ticket takers, etc
- 607 performers
- 300 attend arts and crafts classes
- 200 attend adult drama classes
- 600 attend dance classes
- 700 in Children's Theater
- 555 meetings of outside groups
- 20 art shows (3 with Cleveland Museum of Art, 1 with Cleveland Institute of Art)

In 1988, Fred Sternfeld left the position of artistic director, and for the next two years, there was no artistic director listed in the season playbills. *"There was a two year period after Fred Sternfeld left and Bill Roudebush arrived when we operated without an Artistic Director. There was still the Play Selection Committee, and the General Manager hired the guest directors. It was an interesting time." (Former Technical Director Don McBride)*

An Outreach program was formed in 1988, with a grant from the Gund Foundation, under the direction of Lynda Sackett, to provide arts education with an emphasis on the underserved and at-risk students. "Multicultural Days" were presented with the support of Cox Communications. Thousands of students attended "Arts at Beck Center" (ABC), a half-day program filled with hands-on arts education classes. A financial aid program was established based on need.

Co-Chairs Lucy Sinagra (Lakewood Mayor Tony Sinagra's wife) and Dwayne Cheeks (writer for The Plain Dealer) helped to promote Week-end Jazz Happenings with Billy Eckstein, Jimmy Heath, and other noted jazz artists, along with films, performances, master classes and honorees from the community.

A generous grant from The Gund Foundation in 1988 allowed Beck Center to hire its first Director of Marketing Kerry Kimbrell, and his promotional materials generated enthusiastic responses from the public. The 1988-89 season brochure, "Break a Leg," attracted national attention and was awarded one of only six prizes out of over 750 entries in Target Marketing's 1989 "Best of Direct Marketing Contest."

---

[8] The reported total number of constituents varied over time mainly due to differences in data gathering techniques. Theater audience members were counted every time they attended a performance. Students, however, might have been counted only once per registration for the semester, or they could have been counted for every instance that they were attending classes over numerous weeks. Sometimes constituents were counted that were served out in the community as well as on the Beck campus; sometimes only those on site were counted.

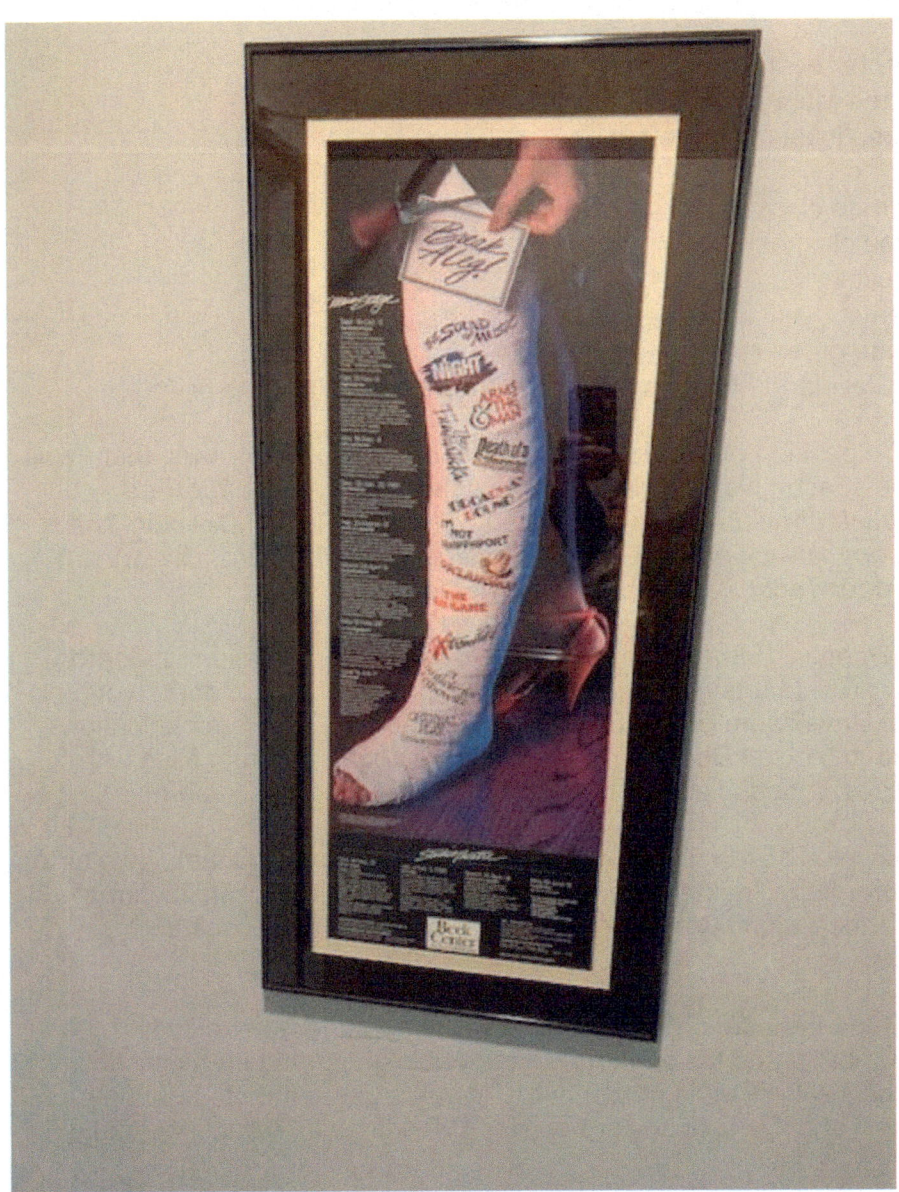

Photo credit Beck Center

In June, 1989, The Plain Dealer reported that The City of Lakewood planned to forgive $90,000 of a $131,522 debt owed by Beck Center for the 1983 land acquisition which included the Armory, deeming it to be a benefit to Lakewood residents. In 1991, the purchase of the Armory was completed by Beck Center.

The bulk of the education programming responsibilities, the Spotlight Series, building utilization, and space rentals were conducted by the team and led by the Founding Director of the Dance Department Lynda Sackett, whose title became Activities Coordinator in 1989.

CUES and VIEWS

The Newsletter of the
Beck Center for the Cultural Arts/Lakewood Little Theatre

VOLUME 10, NO. 1   AUGUST-SEPTEMBER, 1990

Chapin Musical on Main Stage

Beck Center's 1990-91 season will open with an engaging musical that is bound to leave you with a song on your lips and in your heart.

It is "Lies & Legends: the Musical Stories of Harry Chapin," which will be presented as a Greater Cleveland premiere on the Main Stage from Fri.day, Sept. 14 through Oct. 7.

As you can see from the title, this musical revue highlights the songs of the late, popular folk-singer/composer Harry Chapin. It includes his biggest hit, "Taxi," as well as such favorite songs as "Dance Band on the Titanic" and "Cat's in the Cradle."

Chapin was a troubadour of sorts for a couple of generations of pop music fans. When he was killed in an auto accident during 1981, many fans went into mourning. Even now thousands of listeners are drawn to revivals of his "Cotton Patch Gospel," and to concerts honoring him and his music.

Chapin was probably best known for the music he dubbed "story songs," narratives about ordinary people with poignant or unforttunate tales to tell.

A Manhattan native, Chapin was the

was of a big band drummer who played with the Tommy Dorsey band, among others. During the 1960s, Chapin frequently performed in Greenwich Village clubs with his father and two brothers. The family combo also recorded several albums together. In the 1970s, Chapin expanded his musical horizons and became involved with theatre. He received two Tony nominations for a multi-media show and, in 1977, his musical revue played to several cities.

Chapin was also very active in raising funds for a variety of causes, including performing arts centers and campaigns against world hunger.

"Lies & Legends" has been performed in Chicago and New York City during long and critically acclaimed runs. One Chicago Tribune reviewer wrote: "His demise can still move us, his music can still stir us singing." Another reviewer described the show this way: "Clearly evident from the audience's response that if you don't know Chapin's work, you'll love this production. If you do, it will leave your heart and make your

Continued on page 8

MUSIC MAKERS — Appearing in the Greater Cleveland premiere of "Lies & Legends" are Nancy Maier (left), music director; Mickey Houlahan, Ken Benz, and Monica Drake.

[Beck Center registration form]

Acting Class ☐ Art-Craft Class ☐ Children/Teen Theatre ☐ Dance ☐		
COURSE DESCRIPTION	DAY/TIME	INSTRUCTOR

Student Name _____

Address _____ Apt. No. _____

City _____ Zip _____

Home _____ Fax _____ New Student _____

Phone _____ Previous _____

If student is under 18, give age _____ AND parent's name _____

Special needs: Medical _____

Other special needs _____

For Children's Theatre: School, birth date, grade _____

I understand that the Beck Center assumes no liability in the event of accident, injury, or loss of personal property.

Signature of Student _____

OR IF UNDER AGE 18

Signature of parent/guardian _____ DATE _____

Optional, for our Development Office, Employer _____

Tuition $ _____

Supply Fee - $75 _____

Total _____

Cash ☐

Check ☐

Date Paid _____

Charge ☐ _____

Account No. _____

Exp. Date _____

BECK CENTER REGISTRATION POLICY

Tuition is payable IN ADVANCE and is NONREFUNDABLE unless class is canceled because of insufficient enrollment. Assume registration is confirmed unless otherwise notified.

A late fee of $5. will be charged after open registration.

Checks should be made payable to Beck Center. Your canceled check is your receipt.

A limited amount of financial assistance and scholarships are available to students under 18 years of age. Contact the director of the department.

Phonic ear equipment is available for students with hearing impairment.

Studio Season Opens With Prize Winner

A provocative play, by an equally provocative American playwright, will usher in the Studio Theatre season.

The Pulitzer Prize-winning "Buried Child," by Sam Shepard, will be presented in the Studio Theatre from Sept. 28 through Oct. 28.

This challenging and occasionally frenzy work focuses on family ties, and on the myths about the American Dream. It is set in a rather moody farmhouse, occupied by a somewhat unusual family: an alcoholic grandfather, a sometimes grandmother, a son who has lost a leg in a chain saw, and a son who was once an All-American football player but is now a near-idiot.

Their life is interrupted by Vince, a grandson who has come home to visit. Strangely, though, no one seems to recognize or remember him. Vince and the audience, soon discovers that the family harbors a dark secret, one involving a missing infant and a field that suddenly began to grow bumper crops of corn.

"Buried Child" has been praised as "wildly poetic" and "penetrating." A New York Times critic has described Shepard as "one of the most prolific of our young playwrights, and ... certainly one of the most brilliant."

Shepard has written more than 40 plays, almost of which have won Obie Awards. He is the author of "True West," "Lie of the Mind" and "Fool for Love." Fans may recall that Shepard is an actor, too. He received an Oscar nomination for his portrayal of Chuck Yeager in "The Right Stuff." He has also appeared in such movies as "Crimes of the Heart," "Days of Heaven," "Raggedy Man," "Frances" and "Country" (with Jessica Lange).

Scott Spence will direct Beck Center's production.

The Studio Theatre season will con-

(Turn to Pg. 8)

August-September, 1990 – "Cues and Views" newsletter

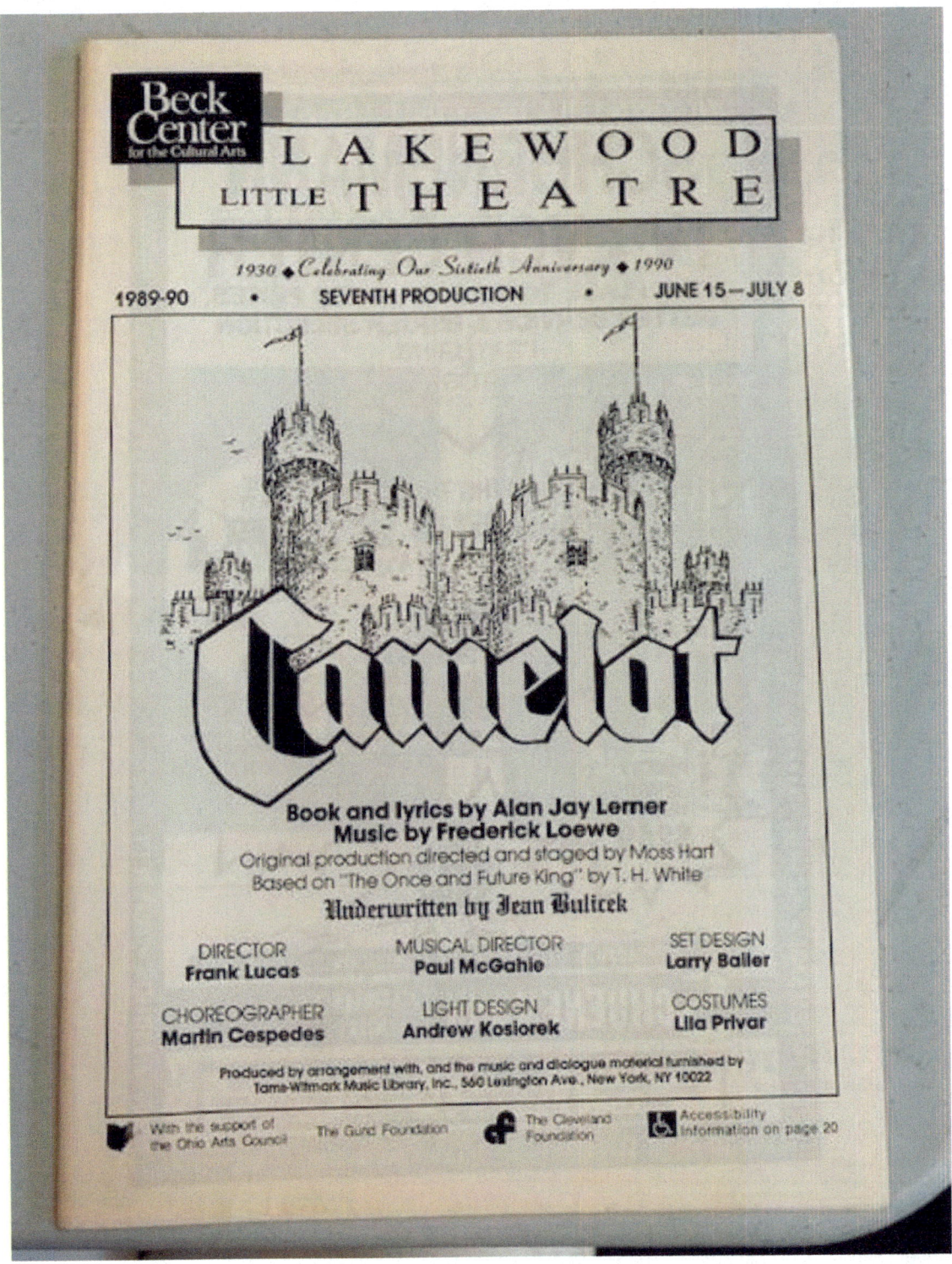

The 1990s were a time of volatility and many leadership changes at Beck Center. Rosemary Corcoran was elected Board President and William Roudebush was hired as Artistic Director in

1990. In 1990, Scott Spence[9] was hired as Associate Artistic Director. Managing Director Faith Killius left the position in 1991, with Andrea Krist taking her place. In 1992, William Roudebush resigned, and Scott Spence was elevated to Artistic Director.

Artistic Director Scott Spence; photo by Wetzler Studios

In keeping with the 1990s, the mission statement was updated in July 1992 to be: "We will create a community where everyone can be directly involved in the performing and visual arts."

April 1992 – Youth Theater Production, Sleeping Beauty – Colin Moeller and Michael Chernus
Photo credit Beck Center

---

[9] See APPENDIX A

Many theater organizations were struggling in the 1990s due to the recession, and the "video culture" also played a part. People who were out of work tended not to go to the theater, but instead would go to a video store and rent a movie for the entire family. Funds to the Ohio Arts Council were cut back substantially due to budget cuts at the state level.

A flow of red ink existed since the main building was enlarged in 1976, and by 1993 there was an annual deficit of about $175,000 from the Center's $1,000,000 annual operating budget. Beck Center was forced to lay off six of 28 employees and consider closing part or all of the former Lucier Theater which housed administrative offices as well as three apartments rented to private tenants. The building had become too expensive to maintain, and tenants were asked to leave after their leases expired. Two of those individuals were Richard Small who occupied the third floor apartment (as of 2022, Beck Archives), and Jerry Macek (as of 2022, the offices of the President & CEO, and finance department employees) who was a talented dance instructor, actor, choreographer, and Education Outreach artist for Beck Center. For a short time (late 1992 to mid-1993), Artistic Director Scott Spence lived in the apartment which as of 2022 houses Beck Center's marketing department.

Beck Center closed for the summer of 1993, and staff cuts were made. This action disabled the marketing and subscription sales for the coming season. Debt to venders increased to $120,000 (about 10% of the operating budget), while the organization struggled to meet payroll as well as mortgage payments and other loan obligations.

The Board conducted a "Survive & Thrive" Strategic Planning process with Consultant Max Stark. One of the focus areas for sustainability was to obtain a firm understanding of the organization's financial status. For many years, audits had been done by the accounting service that Beck Center used in lieu of professional staff. In 1993, an independent accounting firm was hired and that standard practice has continued.

In 1993, Andrea Krist left her position, as did the director of development and director of finance. *"She made her decision that she completed two years at the Beck Center and wanted to do something else,"* said Rosemary Corcoran, President of Beck Center's Board. Ms. Corcoran said that Krist decided to resign over the six-week summer layoff during which the center was closed to save operating money. The Board decided not to replace Ms. Krist immediately but instead to operate the center under team management in cooperation with the trustees. (West Life, September 29, 1993)

January 1993 – Teen Theater Production - *The Snow Queen* – Michael Chernus[10] and James Asmus[11]
Photo credit Beck Center

In 1994, a committee including actor and volunteer archivist Nick Brodella, Board member John Jefferson, Development Director Linda Prosak, Women's Board member Grace Campbell, and freelance writer Ed Walsh, began a project to write a book about the history of Beck Center. Nick Brodella, Lee Ann Curry, Helen Grabner, Dave Schall, and others spent many hours recording and transcribing interviews with dozens of individuals who were instrumental in the growth of the Lakewood Little Theatre. Unfortunately, lack of resources side-lined the project, however, transcripts of these interviews still exist in Beck Center's archives, and many quotes are used in this book.

Rosemary Corcoran assumed the role of general manager 1993 through March of 1994 in addition to her role as Board President (1991-1994). The senior staff was appointed as the Management Team.

In 1994, Lee Parks was elected Board president, and David Pierce was named managing director on January 16, 1995. He acknowledged that he did not have budgeting experience, yet the budget did not allow for the hiring of a finance director. Mr. Pierce came to Beck Center after his role as interim manager of the Ohio Chamber Orchestra, and before that he was executive director of the Cleveland Music School Settlement for almost seven years, and executive director of the Broadway School of Music and the Arts for four years. A graduate of the Baldwin-Wallace Conservatory of Music, he was an accomplished musician who also gave clarinet and recorder lessons out of his Shaker Heights home.

Mr. Pierce hoped to see greater use of the Beck Center's art gallery by poets and musicians. The gallery was at that time home to an artists' cooperative called Visual Harmony where artists display and sell their works. He aspired to be creative in drawing people out, growing the classes for adults and children, and expanding the Children's Theater to a year-round program. *"We've got to have productions to attract people away from sitting at home and being couch potatoes. Live theater and music are facing challenges everywhere these days,"* he said. (West Life, February 15, 1995)

---

[10] As of 2022, Michael Chernus is an accomplished stage actor and 2011 Obie Award winner. He has acted in films such as *Men in Black 3, Captain Phillips, The Bourne Legacy,* and *Jack and Diane.* His most notable role to date is Cal Chapman in the Netflix original comedy-drama series *Orange Is the New Black.*

[11] As of 2022, James Asmus is a writer, actor and comedian known for his affiliation with such theaters as *The Annoyance* and the sketch group *Hey You Millionaires,* and for his work writing comic books such as *Quantum and Woody, Thief of Thieves,* and *Gambit.*

High school student acting now on his future career

By ROGER VOZAR
Staff Writer

It's tough when the downside of your career might be having to appear in a television show or motion picture.

But those are only means to achieving Michael Chernus' ultimate goal of fashioning a career as a stage actor.

The Rocky River High School senior already is ahead of most aspiring thespians by being accepted to the world-renown Julliard Academy in New York City.

He becomes the second recent graduate of the Beck Center School for Children and Teens to enroll at Julliard, following Michael Tisdale, a Lakewood resident and St. Ignatius High School alumnus who will start his second year at Julliard this fall.

The 1,800 applicants to the school's drama department this year included veteran performers and college graduates with theater degrees. Yet Chernus impressed the faculty enough to secure one of 20 spots.

"I started as one of 200 people in a morning audition session," Chernus said. "I didn't think I performed well. It was very intimidating.

"I was surrounded by older people who were very artsy-looking. Here I was, a dorky high school kid. There were a lot of people who thought they were so cool and their faces were all painted. They didn't look like themselves."

Judges liked something they saw in Chernus and called him back for another audition session. Two monologues, one from a Sam Sheppard play and the other from the King Herod role in "Jesus Christ Superstar," convinced the selection panel that he was Julliard material.

"It could be a matter of being what they're looking for," he said. "I know that they want people they can mold into Julliard performers. They also want to build their repertory company. They consider how you look and your style and whether you fit in with what they have.

"I didn't think I had a chance. It shows that you should never give up your dreams."

His dream is to continue presenting the classics, such as a production of Shakespeare's "Much Ado About Nothing" at the Rocky River Recreation Center last August.

Chernus and other Rocky River High School theater students put together the show, including costumes that were comprised partly of 20 jackets purchased at a Goodwill store.

Other credits on his resume include roles in "Lost in Yonkers" at Clague Park, "Oliver" at Lorain County Community College, and Beck Center Teen Theater productions of "The Night Thoreau Spent in Jail" and "The Crucible." Chernus currently is appearing in the Beck Center main stage production of "The Lion in Winter."

Whether it's locally or on Broadway, he wants to remain on the stage, even though he realizes that a four-year degree from the school where Robin Williams and numerous others had their starts could lead to other opportunities.

"They set you up with an agent and make sure that you get work for the first few years," Chernus said. "But I know I'll have to establish a name for myself, if I want to continue."

That's where television and film can help. They may not be as fulfilling, artistically, but they sure can pad the pocketbook.

"Fame and money don't really matter to me. I love the stage. But I'll take work where I can get it, whether it's commercials or film,". Chernus said. "I'll establish myself by working on soap operas if I have to. If I can build myself financially, then I can do what I want.

"I won't lie and say and the fame and money wouldn't make a difference. The money would just make things so much easier. I would enjoy the fame because it means you've gained acceptance. I know actors talk about the pressures of fame but I think I can handle it."

For a high school student, Chernus has a pretty clear vision of his future. But he's already spent years mapping out plans. After being cast in a junior high school production of "The Hobbit," he caught the acting bug and decided this was for him.

As a loner struggling with the difficult early teen years, it was a way to step out of his own character and become someone else.

"I wasn't a child actor. My parents didn't try pushing me into it or anything like that," he said. "I was trying to find something to hook onto' so I wouldn't feel so confused. Even though it was a cheesy junior high play, I felt that I was good and everything. It was something I could feel good about."

When he realized that traditional dramas aren't done that often anymore, he decided to hone his singing and dancing skills.

"I'm a singer and a dancer because I'm an actor," he said. "I never thought of myself as a singer. But I took private voice lessons and I'm in the school show choir. I'm a singer, now."

Local audiences have at least one more chance to see Michael Chernus before he leaves for acting training at the famous Juilliard School in New York. Currently performing in Beck Center's "The Lion in Winter," the high school senior will enroll in Juilliard this fall.

Still, he views many currently popular musicals as spectacles that rely more on flash and gimmicky effects, rather than performing skill.

"I do like some musicals. I love 'Jesus Christ Superstar.' But there's no room in New York for dramas because you have stuff like 'Grease' with Brooke Shields," Chernus said.

While he speaks of places like New York, Chernus hasn't become so struck with the prospects of fame that he's forgotten where he's from.

"You get cocky and forget. For the most part, I haven't," he said.

There are too many obstacles left for him to become too confident. First, he has to come up with $23,000 a year just to attend Julliard, although financial aid will carry some of the burden.

Then, he'll graduate and enter a field crowded with talented people who wind up spending as much time waiting tables as reciting Shakespeare.

"I know it's not going to be glamorous. There's a lot of competition and long hours. It's something I feel I have to do," he said.

"I might end up directing or teaching. But I will be involved in the theater."

March 9, 1995 – Lakewood Sun Post – Beck Alumnus Michael Chernus, © The Plain Dealer. All rights reserved. REPRINTED/USED with permission.

2022 Michael Chernus - Photo credit: Dave Thomas Brown

In 1996, the "Ensure the Future" Capital Campaign was conducted and quickly concluded when a $1,500,000 bequest was received from Helen E. "Betty" Brown, as well as grants from the Cleveland and Gund foundations. These contributions made it possible for Beck Center to pay

Helen "Betty" Brown

its debts, computerize the box office, establish comprehensive budgeting and monitoring systems, reassess fundraising efforts, develop a working capital fund, and establish an endowment. The bequest from Ms. Brown was a surprise to the organization and, indeed, "manna from heaven." Ms. Brown was a lifelong Lakewood resident, and her brother-in-law Jack Timmerman was quoted in Beck Center's *Cues & Views* newsletter, "Betty's gift to Beck Center arose partially from her civic pride and partially from her conviction that Beck Center was a valuable asset to the community. Betty really loved Lakewood, and she always said it was wonderful to have a place like Beck Center – a place for the Arts – right here in her city." The Board of Directors established the Helen Brown Legacy Society in her memory, recognizing those individuals who include Beck Center for the Arts in their will or estate plan.

Managing Director David Pierce noted that expanded education classes were part of Beck Center's plan for long-term financial health and sustainability. Mr. Pierce pointed to statistics that showed students involved in the arts score higher on SATs than those who are not.

The Center's dance workshop trained advanced students who then performed throughout the community. The Metropolitan Opera's create-your-own opera program began, where students learned the entire production process from sets to scripts to ticket sales. Local garage bands received help from Beck Center in finding venues to perform, with three battles of the bands set for 1996.

Goals focused on theater, education and gallery activities. The theater planned eight or nine shows per season, including musicals, dramas and Cleveland premiers of works not yet performed in the area. Beck Center began producing summer musicals in 1996. All were Cleveland premieres of technically difficult and unusual works, i.e., *Chess* (1996) and *Tommy* (1997). *"We're not afraid of going after the impossible projects,"* Mr. Spence said. *"They're the shows no one else in town will touch."*

Youth theater production *Oliver* – photo credit Wetzler Studios

Parents of students in the various departments took active roles helping faculty members. One of those parents, Renata ("Rennie") Tisdale, became the make-up "guru" for the youth theater program in the 1980s. Her sons Michael and Chuck grew up in the Beck Center youth theater program, and they each took on careers in the arts as adults. Ms. Tisdale was hired in 1996 as the registrar for the education department at a time when each department was registering students individually. She centralized/revolutionized the process and eventually became Customer Service Manager. Chuck's son Jake (an employee of Beck Center in both the customer service and finance departments as of 2022) recalls his parents telling him that when he was born, Beck Center's marquee read "Hello, Jake!"

2016 – Cindy Einhouse and Rennie Tisdale; photo credit Beck Center

Teens rock the house

CHUCK CROW / PLAIN DEALER PHOTOGRAPHER

Lutheran High School West sophomore Matt Lillo, left, and Westlake High School junior Dan Benko perform in the Beck Center's production of "Schoolhouse Rock." The musical, based on the educational cartoons televised during the 1970s, ran Sept. 13 through Oct. 6 at the Beck Center. It featured songs such as "Conjunction Junction," "I'm Just a Bill" and "It's Called Verb." This was the Ohio premiere of the play, which featured an adult and youth cast.

HANDY WORK
Ayanna Cash, 6, helped drum up attention for the new ''A Work of Our Hands'' exhibit at Beck Center. An opening festival with drumming, dancing and ethnic foods, was held Saturday to celebrate the intercultural art show. For story, see page A6.

ART

Cleveland Arts Prize show opens at Beck

One of the strongest recent survey exhibitions on contemporary art in Cleveland is coming to the **Beck Center for the Cultural Arts**, 17801 Detroit Ave., Lakewood. On Thursday, the center will open "The Spirit of Cleveland: Visual Arts Recipients of the Cleveland Arts Prize, 1961-1995."

Organized by the Cleveland Institute of Art, the exhibition includes 117 works by 34 artists including Viktor Schreckengost, William McVey, Lilian Tyrrell, Clarence Carter, Shirley Aley Campbell, John Pearson, Athena Tacha, Ed Mieczkowski, Joseph O'Sickey, Julian Stanczak and La Wilson.

The Arts Prize was created in 1960 by Martha J. Joseph and Klaus G. Roy to honor creative achievement in Cleveland. Every visual artist who has won the prize is represented in the exhibition.

The Beck Center display of the show is a return engagement in the Cleveland area. The show debuted at the institute last September, and has since traveled to the Canton Museum of Art, ArtSpace/Lima, and the Riffe Gallery in Columbus.

The show is accompanied by a lavishly illustrated catalog designed by Nesnadny + Schwartz, a Cleveland graphic design firm. The catalog features essays by art collector Michael D. Hall, of Hamtramck, Mich.; and Dennison Griffith, the show's curator, assistant director for programs and planning at the Columbus Museum of Art.

The free exhibition is on view through Oct. 1. Hours are 1 to 6 p.m. Wednesday through Friday. Call 521-2540.

This sterling silver sugar bowl and cream pitcher, made by Frederick A. Miller in 1957 and now in the Cleveland Museum of Art, are in "The Spirit of Cleveland" show.

In 1997, $300,000 was used for capital improvements, and the Board created a $1,200,000 unrestricted endowment that was managed by Fifth Third Bank. John Jefferson was elected Board President. Under David Pierce's direction, the Children's and Teen Theater was expanded to two full semesters with a comprehensive curriculum.

Teaching dance, and life lessons

Lifelong dancer Lynda Sackett, her neck twisting involuntarily, stands before her female students in a mirrored dance studio at the Beck Center for the Cultural Arts in Lakewood. And the music starts.

An estatic smile sweeps across Sackett's face as she and her students sweep across the wooden floor to the soundtrack of the movie "Boogie Nights." Her neck spasms blend in with her movement and seem no longer evident.

On this day, Sackett, who started the dance department at Beck two decades ago, is teaching her "Body Beautiful" class of dance, stretch and endurance exercises to nine students, from their 30s to their 70s.

Like Sackett, whose muscular neck spasms are caused by a neurological disorder, some of the students battle chronic health problems. In her class, they have found inspiration and friendship.

On another day, Sackett, 61, stands before another group, 120 middle school students from Olmsted Falls, who are at Beck for three hours to sample creative dramatics and other arts.

As the just-arrived students yammer in the main theater's seats, she crosses the stage in a tap dance, bringing instant silence and stares. Then clapping.

She tells the students that singing, dancing, pottery and other arts are "a reflection of the way you live."

Sackett has spoken in similar language to more than 15,000 other students from about 25 middle schools who have visited Beck since 1990, when she became the founding director of the center's education outreach program.

Sackett, of Rocky River, also sets up one-day programs in middle schools, including an "African Cultural Sampler" for students to learn about African dance, music, story-telling and other cultural activities.

"By addressing the diversity of our nation we can help to bridge the gaps among our peoples," Sackett says. "Cultural illiteracy is a cause of racism."

Sackett also has set up long-term poetry and play-writing programs in the Cleveland and Elyria schools.

The arts provide ways for students and others "to reach new levels of expression, understanding and awareness," she says.

"In developing a love of the arts it is best to initiate and nurture it in our youth," she says.

In her own youth, Sackett began learning tap dancing at age 4 while growing up in Lakewood. Her family physician recommended she dance to cure a "lazy leg."

She later added ballet to her repertoire but did not start moving her pelvis in dance, she recalls laughing, until the 1950s with the advent of rock 'n' roll.

She graduated from Baldwin-Wallace College with a degree in education and taught elementary school in the Avon Lake and North Olmsted school systems.

But dancing remained integral to her life. She tap danced occasionally in nightclubs and once had her own dance studio in Avon Lake, teaching tap and ballet. In the early 1970s, she was president of the Ballet Guild of Cleveland.

Sackett eventually quit teaching school to raise two sons, but kept up her interest in dance by choreographing children's plays at Lakewood Little Theater, which later became part of Beck Center.

She is past chairwoman of the Lakewood Arts Coalition Steering Committee and is on the board of Nexus, a locally produced interdisciplinary arts magazine.

Sackett was diagnosed with the neurological disorder of dystonia about 20 years ago. She vowed not to let the disorder prevent her from her life's work.

She is continuing to look for ways to improve the art, dance, and outreach programs at Beck.

For the center's next project, she is planning an Arabic Cultural Arts Day at Emerson Middle School in Lakewood next month. It is a pilot program, she says, which she hopes "will help bridge some cultural gaps."

Thomas J. Quinn

HOME COMMUNITY —
Rocky River

AGE — 61

DUTIES — *Dance instructor and arts advocate*

Beck Center and the Cleveland Artists Foundation (CAF) announced that beginning in April 1998, CAF would relocate their visual arts collection to Beck Center's main gallery. CAF's Director Leslie Gibbs said, *"This partnership will broaden the reach, visibility and frequency of our public programs. We are committed to making accessible and preserving regional visual arts which represent our community's history, identity and future, and we now have a perfect location to do so."* (Following the end of its 10 year lease, CAF changed its name to ArtNEO and moved to 78th Street Studios in the Gordon Square neighborhood.)

In 1998, a committee of the Board and staff worked with planning consultant Patricia Doyle on goals that included building a $1,000,000 endowment, reconfiguring the space within the center more effectively, strengthening and enlarging education and volunteer programs and developing collaborations with other institutions. Unfortunately, the goal for the endowment was not met, and in fact a portion of the existing endowment had to be used for operations. In 1998, David Pierce left his position, and Lisa Nespeca was hired as Managing Director.

Colleen Lanning and Connie Smialek followed in the individualized teaching culture established by Jan Egert, and then in 1998, Lynette Gutman became the new Children's Theater and Teen Theater director for the Center. Events took place to celebrate the 50th anniversary of its children's theater programs. Catherine York-Norris, a graduate of the New England Conservatory of Music and formerly guest composer at Cornell University in Ithaca, New York was appointed resident music director, a new staff position. Beck Center was the first theater in Ohio to perform *Spider Woman*, adapted from Manuel Puig's novel and the film made from it.

January 1998 – new signage installed

January 1998 – installation of new marquee

In 1999, the endowment continued to erode, and Ms. Nespeca left the position, however, faculty and staff managed to continue strong programming. Beginning with the 1998-99 season, as part of a new strategic plan, Beck Center began paying stipends to each of its actors. This change provided opportunities to draw from a wider pool, become eligible for membership in the Professional Alliance of Cleveland Theaters (PACT), choose from a larger selection of titles, and provided greater visibility in the main Cleveland newspaper *The Plain Dealer*.

Beck Center experimented with taking education programming out into the community, performing youth theater production *Fairy Tales Tonight* at Brunswick United Methodist Church in 1999, and offering a Theater Apprentices Summer Workshop at the Schaaf Community Center in Parma in 1999. Collaborations included participating with Playhouse Square in an entire season of *Broadway Buzz* presentations and cast workshops at Beck Center.

Patricia Sigmier joined the Visual Arts faculty in 1999 and as of 2022 is one of the longest-time members of that department, teaching a wide variety of classes over the years related to painting and water color. She has countless devotees who take her weekday painting classes, including those new to painting and those who continue to develop their artistic skills. She has been featured in Beck Center art exhibitions over the years, and her artwork has been in galleries across Northeast Ohio.

Also in 1999, Rachel Spence joined the Theater Education faculty, eventually becoming Associate Director of Outreach Education until the pandemic forced the discontinuation of her role in 2020. As of 2022, Ms. Spence continues to serve Beck Center in numerous capacities, including teacher, actor, director, and playwright. She has directed and/or written dozens of productions for students.

"Find a job that you love, and you'll never work a day in your life." – Rachel G. Fox's advice to Beck Center students, Feb 2011

Rachel G. Fox – photo source IMDb.com

Beck Alumna Rachel G. Fox came to Beck Center on February 26, 2011 to share her story after the staging of Beck Center's Teen Theater production *Into the Woods,* directed by Jonathan Kronenberger. First appearing on stage in the Beck Center Youth production "Santa Goes Commercial," (2007) Rachel then earned stage roles at several local venues. A family trip to Los Angeles and a stint at a summer acting camp led to her TV appearances on "iCarly," "Passions," "Hannah Montana" and a role in prime time as Kayla Huntington on "Desperate Housewives."

CHAPTER 9:
Evolving to Professional – 2000-2020

In 2000, as Lakewood organization Riverside Music Academy (formerly Koch School of Music) struggled to survive, the Boards came together to implement a merger with Beck Center, and thus the Music & Creative Arts Therapies program (which Riverside had founded in 1994) moved into the Armory on the Beck campus. Henry Holtkamp had been elected Board President 1999, following John Jefferson, and William Beckenbach became Managing Director in 2000.

Completed in 2001, the merger with Riverside brought highly dedicated and talented teachers to Beck Center, including:

- Certified music therapist Ed Gallagher,[12] who became director of education and Creative Arts Therapies, and then director of education. Creative Arts Therapies became a full program within the education department, and Mr. Gallagher became one of Beck Center's longest time employees.
- Christopher Ellicott, who became a faculty member in Beck Center's music education department, teaching guitar, electric bass, and ukulele, and remains on the faculty as of 2022.
- Bruce Erwin, who began teaching at Riverside in 1992 and continued in the music department teaching violin at Beck Center until his retirement in 2017. He performed in the Fort Worth Symphony Orchestra, the Canton Symphony Orchestra, the AIMS Orchestra in Graz, Austria and La Orquesta Sinfonica de Xalapa in Mexico. He compiled and edited a collection of fiddle tunes from the Scottish tradition called The Fiddler's Wrist, published by FJH Music in 2003.
- Vilma Vargo, certified in Dalcroze Eurhythmics from Carnegie-Mellon University, who taught children as young as three years old the joy of learning the fundamentals of music through movement for over 50 years. Ms. Vargo continued to teach at Beck Center up until she passed away in 2020.
- Judi Votypka, who started at Riverside in 1991 in administration and played an important role in implementing the merger between Riverside and Beck Center in 2001. Throughout the years after, she served as head of the music program, administrator in the education department, and education account manager in the finance department before retiring in 2018.

2018 - Creative Arts Therapies student at Sensory Friendly Halloween Trick or Treat

With $500,000 of funding from the State of Ohio in 2000, the Armory Building was remodeled to house Beck Center's Conservatory of Music, and capital improvements were made to other buildings. A fundraising gala called "Beckcitement" raised $35,000, and the funds were used for operations and building maintenance. Faculty/student recitals and children's choir concerts were offered to the community free of charge.

In 2001, Ron Waldheger was elected Board President. Stock market conditions eroded the endowment. Volunteers stepped up to make sure that faculty and students had the resources they needed to run successful programs.

---

[12] See APPENDIX A

In 2003, Bill Beckenbach resigned, and Elizabeth Horrigan was hired as the new Executive Director. There were still no funds available to hire a chief financial officer. With $100,000 of funding from the State of Ohio, the patron service area was expanded, as well as public restrooms; painting and capital improvements gave the public spaces an atmosphere of a successful operation. Strategic decisions were made to elevate skills and giving capacity of the Board.

In 2004, payables were at $180,000 (18% of the operating budget), and the endowment was depleted. Significant efforts were initiated to establish partnerships with arts and education organizations. Meetings began with lending institutions to explore long term financing. In an effort to more clearly define the roles of Board President and the Executive Director, the titles were changed to Chairman of the Board and President & CEO. The staff received 15% salary cuts, and this action resulted in many long-time education faculty members leaving Beck Center.

In 2005, Ron Waldheger resigned as Board Chair and as a Board member. Rosemary Corcoran was elected Board Chair. Cleveland Foundation provided a grant of $200,000 to stabilize the organization, provide funds for an experienced financial consultant, and determined that the services of a turn-around consultant were mandatory. A matching annual fund campaign yielded $50,000, and the Board increased its giving.

Jim Walton assumed the role of consultant and Chief Financial Officer. After a thorough analysis, Mr. Walton found the past due bills to be over 40% higher than what was reflected in the accounting records, the Worker's Compensation Insurance lapsed, and the necessity to recreate the general ledger before the very laborious 2003/04 audit process could be completed. New surprises awaited him every day. The 2005/06 budget was balanced and would be approved quarterly by the Board.

The John P. Murphy Foundation provided a grant for marketing and for Community Partners Consulting, the turn-around specialists. Reporting to the Board, Howard Parr and Janus Small conducted this process from September 2005 through February 2006 and provided a report stressing the importance of both arms of the programming – theater and arts education – and their strengths. They also include a series of recommendations, including 1) re-aligning the staff structure, and hiring a highly qualified CEO who would oversee all programs recognizing that theater and education are equally important to the overall function and service; 2) fully integrating all aspects of public relations and marketing across all programming areas, 3) clarifying the Beck message (brand), and 4) requiring 100% Board participation in annual fundraising.

Board discussions continued about education and artistic partnership. An ad hoc committee of the Board was formed to discuss the redevelopment of the campus into a more affordable facility rather than a sprawling, aging campus.

Elizabeth Horrigan left her position in October 2005, and Jim Walton assumed the additional role of Interim Executive Director as a full-time employee. An Audit Committee of the Board was established as a permanent committee. Fred Unger was elected Chairman, while the management team, faculty, and staff did remarkable work providing programming with very few resources.

In an article in The Plain Dealer on September 18, 2005, theater critic Tony Brown described Artistic Director Scott Spence as "…*the Cleveland area's current chutzpah champ. But this season, he appears to have outdone himself. He's just opened 'Urinetown the Musical,' to be followed two weeks hence with Suzan-Lori Parks' 'Top Dog/Underdog,' an in-your-face drama no other theater in town would touch. Crazy? Perhaps. But he's sly enough to also have the commercially promising 'Beauty and the Beast' and 'The Full Monty' on tap, and they're pretty darn ambitious, to boot. Stay crazy, Scotty."*

Beck Center began 2006 with a firm grasp of the financial realities, and the 15% salary cuts were restored. While the Community Partners Consulting report found Beck Center to be strong in programming and in staff competency, the Center had been operating at a $200,000 - $500,000 annual deficit for many years, thus the erosion of the endowments.

At this time, Board leadership was approached by a developer to consider moving the entire organization to leased space at Crocker Park in Westlake. However, there was a strong sentiment from citizens of Lakewood as well as a suggested collaboration with the Lakewood City School District that ultimately influenced a decision to stay. The proposed collaboration, initiated by then Superintendent of the Lakewood City School District Dr. David Estrop, was an Arts & Communications Academy for high school students interested in developing professional skills in the arts.

In addition, an economic impact study by Impact Economics determined Beck Center's location in Lakewood was ideal. The study determined that Beck Center, serving about 45,000 people per year in 2006, had an annual economic impact of $10 million in Cuyahoga County due in great part to vendor and visitor spending. The Board recommitted to the site, which at that time consisted of three buildings, front courtyard and adjacent parking on 3 ½ acres.

A very significant development occurred in May of 2006 when a major Cleveland financial institution became a key partner in Beck's future, National City Bank. The bank provided a $1,000,000, 20-year mortgage to eliminate past accounts payable, pay down several lines of credit, and leave some funds to handle cash flow issues.

Cleveland Foundation convened the major foundations in 2006 so that Beck Center could request $600,000 to support the turn-around plan and stabilization through 2008. With this support, a strategic planning process and executive search for the President & CEO took place in 2006.

Planning began for the 75th anniversary season and various celebrations in 2006-2007. A marketing and development newsletter was created as a means of ongoing communication with constituents and donors. A major donor focused fundraising effort began.

Clay tile mural, by visual arts camp students; photo credit Beck Center

Intrigued by the sudden notoriety of Beck Center because of the news of its decision to stay in Lakewood rather than moving to Crocker Park in Westlake, Lakewood resident Lucinda (Cindy) Einhouse[13] joined the Board of Beck Center in 2006. At that time, she had just completed managing a successful capital campaign for the Cleveland Institute of Music and had some time to invest in the Lakewood community, where she had lived since 1980. Board President Fred Unger asked Ms. Einhouse to be on the committee to search for the organization's first President/CEO in its newly structured administration.

After recommending to the committee what she thought were well-qualified candidates for the position, Mr. Unger surprised her by saying the committee was "actually most interested in you" because of her professional fundraising background, MBA degree, and educational background in music and theater. During the previous several months as a member of the Board, Ms. Einhouse had become well aware of the dire needs of the organization, including $1,250,000 in debt, over $600,000 in past due payables, and about $5 in the checking account. She also knew that the culture of philanthropy of the organization was very grassroots and subsisted primarily on foundation grants, so it was in no position to begin a capital campaign without the proper infrastructure. There were three different phone numbers for each of the three buildings on the Beck campus, and the phone system didn't have a working message system. The IT server for the organization was so old that an employee had to hit it with a tap shoe in the morning to make it work. No more than about a dozen emails could be sent out at one time without crashing the computer system.

In spite of all that, Artistic Director Scott Spence and Education Director Ed Gallagher and their teams were managing wonderful programs with exceptionally little resources in the budget, so it was no wonder that the organization obviously mattered greatly to the patrons and students. Thinking back to her college aspiration of running an arts organization someday, Ms. Einhouse accepted the position and began May 1, 2007 as President & CEO.

---

[13] See APPENDIX A

2012 – Lucinda (Cindy) Einhouse

Photo credit Beck Center

Rather than making changes in the staffing or organizational structure, Ms. Einhouse focused her efforts on reconnecting Beck Center with the community. The outside appearance of an organization impacts how others view an organization's culture, just like how the clothing a person wears may cause people to make assumptions about them.

This photo from 2007, demonstrates the modest, unassuming architecture of the 1970s. The dark, recessed front entrance and lack of windows on the front of the building made the organization look uninviting to the neighborhood and gave no indication of the vibrant, exciting programming going on inside. Thus, Beck Center was known as a "best kept secret."

Annex building at Rockway and Detroit Avenues, 2008; photo credit Beck Center

For many years, the façade was utilitarian, plain, and uninspiring. Sheets were draped over the front windows of the classrooms facing Detroit Avenue to hide stock piles of storage items. The marquee had ceased to function, giving the appearance the entire place was closed. There were extremely limited funds available for print advertising, and electronic communication was limited due to lack of technology.

"Best kept secret" translated into very limited potential for both earned and contributed revenue. As the new CEO, Ms. Einhouse focused efforts on increasing the visibility and engagement of the community with Beck Center's creative, exciting programs. She began an annual collaboration with The Lakewood/Rocky River Rotary[14] to help clean up landscaping every fall and spring.

---

[14] The Lakewood/Rocky River Rotary has had a long association with the organization and in the past, held its meetings at Beck Center. For many years, Beck Center has collaborated with the Rotary on an annual Music, Speech and Visual Arts Contest for high school students in Lakewood and Rocky River. As of 2022, the Rotary continues to provide generous cash prizes while Beck Center provides administrative support, judges, promotional materials, and space for exhibits and the awards ceremony.

She engaged good friend and international art dealer Paul Sykes to donate four colorful and expressive murals for the outside walls, creating the largest outdoor mural museum in the region. Mr. Sykes also invested his own money in transforming one of the storefronts into the Beck Café - a combination art gallery/music venue/coffee shop with a wall fountain and a koi fish pond under a Plexiglas ramp. (Mr. Sykes operated the Beck Café from 2008 through 2012, before moving his business to Florida.)

In 2007, when Lynda Sackett retired from directing the dance department, Melanie Szucs assumed the position of Associate Director of Dance Education. Ms. Sackett continued to teach dance classes at Beck Center until her full retirement in 2019. Part of the strength of the Dance Department was and is due to the talent, dedication, and longevity of its faculty. The number of years Lynda Sackett, Melanie Szucs, Joan Hartshorne and Mimi Schwensen[15] collectively served at Beck Center totaled over 160 as of 2022 and still counting. Ms. Hartshorne taught creative and modern dance until her retirement in 2019, and Ms. Szucs and Ms. Schwensen continue to inspire students to expand their horizons and talents at Beck Center while embracing their love of dance. Many Beck students went on to major in dance in college, including Ali Cassidy who graduated from Ohio State University and Abby Viscomi who graduated with a bachelors and masters in dance from Kent State University. They were among the first Beck alumni to teach dance at Beck Center.

2015, "Night at the Opera" mural by Natasha Turovsky, donated by Paul Sykes; photo credit Beck Center

---

[15] Mimi Schwensen, a former Rockette, joined the Dance faculty in 1985. She has worked with Melanie Szucs for all of the holiday and spring shows and assisted in evaluating students who audition for productions. She has also traveled with the dance department to Columbus each year for the OhioDance Festival and prior to that to the Youth America Grand Prix (YAGP) regionals in Chicago and Pittsburg, rehearsing the company students as a volunteer. YAGP is the world's largest non-profit international student ballet competition and scholarship program, open to dance students of all nationalities, 9–19 years old.

2004 - Annie Gagen backstage after Dance Recital

2021 – Annie Gagen in Christmas Wonderland – Reno, NV
Photo credit: @lostprincessproductions and @asian_david@alleykerr

Beck dance student Annie Gagen graduated from Point Park University with a BA in Dance and a Minor in Musical Theatre. From there, she began performing at theme parks and on cruise ships, including the Norwegian Cruise Lines. She visited over 50 different countries all the while singing Broadway classics, Viennese waltzing, and rocking out to Queen. She had this to say in 2021:

"I began taking classes at Beck Center in 1997 when I was five years old and my mother enrolled me in the S.M.I.L.E. class. From there, I moved on to pre-ballet and ballet, and then added tap and jazz into the mix. I had Mrs. Szucs for most (if not all) of my ballet classes until Anna Roberts joined the faculty. I had Lynda Sackett and Mimi Schwensen for tap and Mrs. Szucs (and, at the tail end of my time at Beck, Lou Hadaway) for jazz! Some of my best and most vivid memories are of doing Dance Workshop Nutcrackers and going to the NEO Dance Festival to take a full day of master classes and then perform with my best friends. I also took Youth Theatre classes and was a part of many Main Stage shows at the Beck, my favorite being Hairspray in 2011."

The Growing Importance of Technology
In 2008, Ms. Einhouse encouraged one of Beck Center's most loyal and generous supporters Virginia Foley to make a special gift to fund the installation of a new state-of-the-art digital marquee. The highly skilled and dedicated Beck Center management team fully embraced the priority to engage the community and make the programming visible.

Photo credit Beck Center

Technology was proving to be very critical to the business, especially after the computer server ceased to function in 2005, and all previous data was lost since no back-up files existed. Software for selling tickets and keeping track of class registrations was so old that vendors no longer provided support when needed. In 2008, members of the Beck theater orchestra Larry Goodpaster[16] and Karen Langenwalter volunteered their time to research the business and made recommendations on appropriate vendors for ticket and class registration software.

Public support of the arts had never before been organized in Cuyahoga County, but it happened just in time before the country's economic recession of 2008. Residents created Cuyahoga Arts & Culture in 2006 when they voted to approve a tax on cigarettes to support arts and culture. As of 2022, Cuyahoga Arts & Culture (CAC) has become one of the largest local public funders for arts and culture in the nation, helping hundreds of organizations in Cuyahoga County connect millions of people to cultural experiences each year. Beck Center received its first annual allocation of funding in 2007 when the organization was in financial crisis, and as of 2022 has received a total of over $2.4M from this critical source. In fact, as of this writing, CAC has the largest cumulative giving of any donor in Beck Center's history. It is safe to say that Beck Center would not still be in business if not for this vital public support.

The State of Ohio also has provided critical support through the Ohio Arts Council – a total of more than $1,500,000 to Beck Center throughout the years, in addition to over $500,000 in total appropriations from the Capital Budget for renovations of the buildings, as of 2022.

Philanthropic support has been transformational to the organization over the recent decades, in stark contrast to the early decades where the leadership prided itself on "never asking anyone for anything." Thanks to volunteer Patrick Reymann who became a valuable business advisor to Ms. Einhouse, Beck Center received support from the Jean Thomas Lambert Foundation in 2008 and was able to purchase computer hardware and software which greatly increased the

---

[16] See APPENDIX A

organization's technological capability. This improved technology allowed for the development of an electronic database which quickly grew to thousands of constituents (over 12,000 in 2022) and eventually a lively social media presence which was critical to selling theater tickets and class registrations.

In 2010, the Lambert Foundation, at the encouragement of Mr. Reymann, funded the redesign of Beck Center's website, which led to a significant increase in theater revenue within the first year. The website also brought a new and improved look to the online newsletter, *ArtsLine*.

Razzle Dazzle production, in cooperation with the Cuyahoga County Board of Developmental Disabilities Photo credit Beck Center; collaborative partners for over 20 years

Red Stage concert; photo credit Beck Center

As print advertising had become cost prohibitive, a social media presence was essential to spread the word about arts education, performances, exhibitions and outreach. Previously, individual programs had been promoted, however, there had not been an effort to market the institution as a whole. New branding language and a "brand promise" were developed, with an institutional priority: To create entry points for people to an arts experience.

Ed Gallagher leading "Super Saturday" activities; photo credit Beck Center

Entry points to an arts experience included a free Summer Music Series in the front yard funded by The Callahan Foundation and the annual "Bike for Beck" bicycle ride (which took place 2012 through 2016) with interactive activities for children and families, showing off Beck Center's proximity to the MetroParks trailhead.

Renewing a Long-Time Commitment to Inclusion and Engagement
Recognizing that diversity, equity, and inclusion are essential to the organization, Ms. Einhouse enrolled Beck Center for the Arts as a member of the Commission on Economic Inclusion in January, 2010. Membership meant committing to participate in an annual employer's survey on diversity and studying best practices in organizational leadership on diversity and inclusion. The following year, in May 2011, Beck Center received The Commission 50 designation which recognized 50 organizations (25 for-profit, 25 non-profit/government) with the highest combined scores on Board, senior management, workforce and supplier diversity on the Commission's Employers Survey on Diversity.

Area foundations were leading the way in diversity, equity, and inclusion (DEI) training, not only because it was the right thing to do, but because organizations needed to think about how they were attracting the audiences of the future. In 2011, as part of the Cleveland Foundation's "Engaging the Future" initiative, Beck Center's Executive Committee met, discussed, and committed to embracing racial and ethnic diversity, as well as diversity of sexual orientation.

Beck at "Parade the Circle"; photo credit Beck Center

Beck Center committed to reach out to broader, more diverse communities. For many years, faculty, staff, and volunteers participated in University Circle's "Parade the Circle," with large creative pieces that fit the theme of the year, led by the Visual Arts department along with people from the community. The team then participated in Lakewood's July 4 parade and won "Most Creative Entry" ten years in a row before deciding to fund the prize for other organizations to win.

Inner courtyard; photo credit Beck Center

Beck Center began to lose its modesty and get better at telling the story about the many ways in which children and adults can engage in arts experiences. Staff and faculty had always been incredibly committed to students and patrons, like a family. Every opportunity was embraced to convey the organizational values of warmth and engagement. When a duck (which the staff named "Becky") came several years in a row to lay eggs in the inner courtyard, patrons and students were welcomed to come in, see an art exhibition, and visit Becky and her family.

Ms. Einhouse began a regular online communication to faculty, staff, and volunteer leaders called the *Beck Family Update*, providing the inside scoop, updates, and accomplishments. The organization has maintained an unpretentious and authentic personality which resonates with many students and patrons.

2011 - Counter-protestors – "Jerry Springer, The Opera"; photo credit Beck Center

In 2011, Artistic Director Scott Spence produced *Jerry Springer, The Opera*, starring Gilgamesh Taggett as Satan, and Matthew Wright as Jerry Springer. The Board – chaired by Mary Kim Elkins at that time - was alerted that other venues across the country had experienced protests against the production due to what some felt to be sacrilegious content. The piece is a critically-acclaimed and innovative approach to musical theater – the type of piece which attracts very talented actors. Audiences were alerted to the satirical, potentially provocative nature of the production, and it indeed spurred ticket sales.

Beck Center was the top news story on every local television station on opening night when a fundamentalist group based in Kansas and Pennsylvania staged a major protest of the show, perceiving some elements of the show to be an attack on Catholicism. Nearly 20,000 emails were triggered by the group to Ms. Einhouse, Ms. Elkins, Lakewood Mayor Michael Summers, Cleveland Foundation President Ronn Richard, and Gund Foundation President David Abbott. Responses of support for Beck Center were sent from each. Beck Center also received many messages of appreciation and philanthropic contributions from those who attended the production.

A talk-back was scheduled after one of the productions to talk about censorship of the arts, including Mr. Abbott and Dennis Barrie, former Director of the Cincinnati Contemporary Arts Center (CCAC) from 1983-1992. Mr. Abbott reinforced the Foundation's position on supporting the arts while not judging artistic choices. Mr. Barrie spoke about his experience in 1990 when he and CCAC were indicted and acquitted on obscenity charges stemming from exhibiting sadomasochistic photographs by Robert Mapplethorpe as part of an exhibit entitled *The Perfect Moment*.

"Under Jenniver Sparano's direction, I made all of the KKK robes for 'Jerry Springer.' Interesting resume addition for a lifelong card-carrying liberal!" – Janice Mastin-Kamps, Women's Board member

photo credit Jenn Cassidy

Beck staff and faculty strive for a high level of professionalism - a balance of professionalism and fun, in a comfortable non-rigid environment. Accessibility and engagement are priorities.

Photo credit Wetzler Studios   *Photo credit Beck Center*

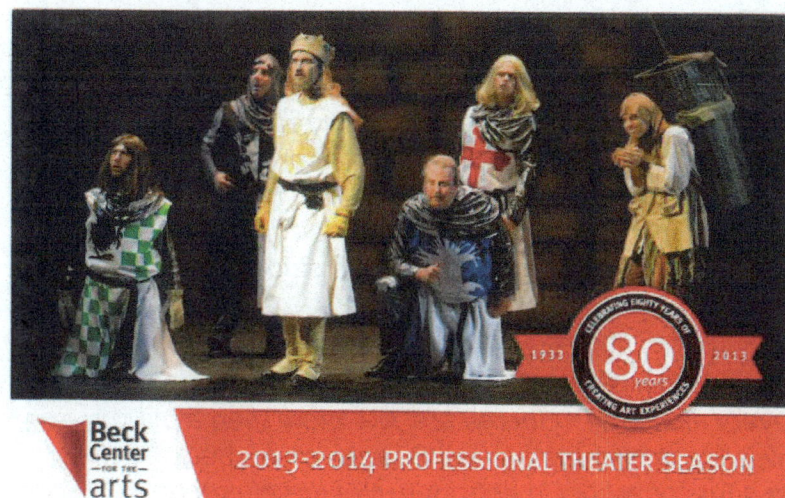

2013 – "Avenue Q," Youth Theater production; photo credit Wetzler Studios

The Beck Effect

"After my car accident, they took a chance on me before I even learned how to walk again. Beck Center saved my life." – Adriana Holst, theater student

"Beck Center is unique in that I can drop my daughter off for dance instruction in the morning; that afternoon, Beck will go out into the community and deliver art experiences to different community groups; and at night, my wife and I can see a professional theater production." – Tom Fraser, CEO, First Mutual Holding Co.

"Thank you to Beck Center and all of the donors that are a part of making this possible for my children." – Gwendolyn David, parent

"I loved working with the clay. It felt squishy in my hands and that made me feel really relaxed. Working with all the different tolls with their edges and sharp points made me feel grown up. I could decorate my clay with squiggly lines and different shapes. I could create anything I wanted with anyone telling me what to make or how to make it. All the different colors were so interesting because they turned different when they went into the kiln. Plus the colors are just plain beautiful! I loved the freedom of making things out of clay! Most of all, I loved the fact that the teacher always respected everyone's art." – Una Bryson, visual arts student

"Beck Center is my second home. Every teacher shows enough support to single-handedly convince you that you could fly; and every moment I'm there I feel like more than a million bucks. Beck Center is what I love, and is something that I never wish to leave. Beck Center keeps me going throughout the boring hours of school in anticipation of the afternoon rehearsals, weekend shows, and Saturday classes. I never want summer to end so that the

camps can last forever, but can't wait for the next theater season. My favorite moment is almost impossible to pick out, because any moment I'm at Beck is a favorite moment. The Beck is the best place for me, and I hope to come for much longer." – Lucy Kress, student

"From the moment I quietly stepped into the Beck Center, I knew that it would be a place that would greatly change my life for the better. And it was from that moment where I knew that I would fall in love with the atmosphere, teachers, and people. I also knew right off the bat, I would make relationships and memories that would be embedded in my heart forever…Every time I step into Beck Center for the Arts, I come to a place that I can call home, and most importantly, be with my family." – Matt Fox, student

September 6, 2011

Dear Cindy,

I have wanted to write a letter now for years to the Beck Center to communicate the admiration and gratitude our family has for the staff and all those who make the Beck such an outstanding part of our community.

Did I first put that letter on my 'to do' list over 9 years ago when Eva and I enrolled in "Kids-N- Tunes"? Or, was it after she took her first ballet class about 8 years ago? Maybe it was when Jack finished Dalcroze. I'm not sure, but it was still on my list this summer when Jack finished his art camp with the confidence of Jackson Pollock, and I got some Cuban motion in Zumbalates class with the delightful Ms. Anna.

Our first encounter with the Beck Center was in 2001 with Mr. Ed in the Kids-N-Tunes class. I desperately needed human contact and to get out of the house after Jack was born. Eva was 2, and Jack was a newborn in a car seat. I was uneasy that day, on the way to the first class. Here's the dialogue that went on in my head: "Oh, he's going to cry the entire class and make everyone miserable and the instructor will remind me that *Eva* is the student enrolled in the class, and I shouldn't be bringing Jack. But, I am going crazy staying home and so is she. We need to get out and do something." And on and on and on.... Oh, how lucky was I that this class was taught by the devoted man that I would later see daily in the halls of the Beck Center (and as an usher and sound man at Beck events, as a puppeteer in the Fourth of July parade, selling concessions at evening performances, etc , etc). During our class (and every time we saw him outside of class- which was often- does the guy live there?), Mr. Ed was smiling and kind and attentive and patient. Eva loved the class, and so did I. At that first class, when Mr. Ed put maracas in Jack's hands, I knew I had found a place of peace and support and learning for my family. Mr. Ed suggested the pre-ballet class for Eva, and the rest is history. But, I really must share some of that history....

Eva hit the recital stage the summer of 2003 at the age of 4 dressed as a bunny and holding a carrot. Well, she hit the stage, but immediately froze, and started to cry uncontrollably. Very soon after, Ms. Szucs came out on stage, put her arms around Eva and carried her off to the arms of her alarmed mother. Eva would not give up the tutu easily and wanted to re-enroll in the fall. She has been a dance student for every session since. Every showcase, every recital, and many times in between, I watch Melanie Szucs share her amazing talents with her students and marvel at the Beck Center's good fortune to have such an outstanding teacher in our midst. I remember sitting in the Mackey Main Stage seats during a dance recital rehearsal a few years ago, and listening to Melanie Szucs provide direction to class after class after class. I listened to her calm, reassuring tone. I noted that she addressed every dancer by name; from the toddlers to the adults. I remember thinking I should write a letter.....

Since 2003, I have wept at every dance recital, every showcase, every 'parent visitation' day. I remember my daughter as the scared little bunny, comforted by her dear teacher. I am certain without the care and support Eva has received from Ms. Szucs all these years, Eva would not be dancing today. She would not be, at the age of 11, reading "Dance" magazine and planning which college she will attend to receive her dance major. Later this month, Eva will receive her first pair of pointe shoes, and she is ecstatic. It's no surprise that Melanie Szucs will sacrifice her Saturday afternoon to be there to provide guidance to all her dancers as they make their selections.

We are so very fortunate to have such a place of talent and creativity. A place where there is something for everyone- for those of us who have never held a paint brush, put on a pair of tap shoes, or picked-up an instrument. For those of us whose dream it is to be a prima ballerina or a professional musician. For those of us who just need to get out the house and shake some maracas!

Thank you Cindy, for all that you do to make the Beck Center the place that it is. I am forever grateful to the teachers, especially Ed Gallagher and Melanie Szucs, who have added so much to my family's life.

Sincerely,

Jen Wynn

Letter to Lucinda (Cindy) Einhouse from a parent of students – Jen Wynn – September 6, 2011

Speech by Creative Arts Therapies student Suzanne Hardy to public officials in Columbus, at Beck Center's "Hill Day" 2017:

Thank you for inviting me to this event. I hope this little speech gives you a better idea of the type of students the Beck Center helps. My name is Suzanne Hardy. I am 27 years old and was born with a genetic syndrome called Williams syndrome.

Unfortunately, I have many physical and learning disabilities. I can look up anything on a computer, but asking me to add numbers is very difficult. I would be great at the old show, Name that Tune, and I'm great at remembering people. When I was around 13 years old, I started taking music and art therapy lessons at the Beck Center. The therapists were inspirational and did their best at trying to get me to express myself. I gained confidence and started talking more. I am always afraid of saying the wrong thing. I worry that people will not like me because of my disabilities.

Several years ago, I out grew the type of lessons offered at the Beck. Mr. Gallagher got me involved helping out at the Rock Hall Head Start Music group on Tuesday mornings. I enjoy working with the young children. I can teach the alphabet and sing with the Rock band. This experience has helped me to be more outgoing and conversational. I do not think the children or staff of the Rock Hall see me as having a disability.

I joined Razzle Dazzle about 8 years ago. I was quiet and shy but got to know the other cast members and the crew. I admire the crew because they have made all of us feel that when we are practicing and performing we do not have disabilities. The crew helps guide us on and off the stage; they make sure we are headed in the right direction. Sometimes, we twirl around instead of taking a bow. Ann (Huebner) helps guide us with arm motions in the back behind the audience. One of my favorite parts of the show is when the audience joins in the conga line. Sometimes people are reluctant to get out of their seats; but those that do have a fun time and laugh a lot as they conga around the room.

We look forward to our Wednesday night practices. We share our lives and the crew shares theirs. The Razzle group are true friends. Razzle Dazzle has helped all of us become more confident, more spontaneous, and more alive.

I hope that Razzle and the Beck Center Art and Music therapies will always be there for us. I hope that other communities will start Razzle programs for other people with disabilities. Thank you for supporting Art and Music Therapy at The Beck Center.

2017 – Suzanne Hardy speaking to public officials in Columbus, Ohio; photo credit Beck Center

2016 – Graphic Design and Marketing Coordinator Patrick Miller, Associate Director of Visual Arts Darrelle Centuori, Associate Director of Outreach Education Rachel Spence; photo credit Patrick Miller

The staff and faculty are creative and committed, and they bring their own sense of style to everything they do. A number of Beck Center employees formed a band to perform on occasion for young audiences.

Photo credit Beck Center

Since so many students are aged 12 and under, faculty and staff are extremely attentive to maintaining an inclusive, safe, developmentally appropriate and fun environment. Every opportunity is taken to reinforce the values of honesty, transparency, and professionalism with everyone who comes into contact with the students.

A collaborative and team-oriented environment is important to the staff, realizing that more can be accomplished working together than in silos of operation. In 2016, staff drafted a "Beck Synergy" pact which is a promise to each other to strive for positive work life. And in 2019, "Safe Zone" training was provided to all staff and faculty by the LGBT Center of Cleveland, to help enlighten and heighten sensitivity to needs of individuals with different identities and orientations.

BECK Synergy
Our Promise to Each Other

April 2016

1. We will treat everyone fairly and with respect.

2. We will be considerate of each other's ideas and opinions, and receptive to change.

3. We will help and support others to effectively do their job.

4. We will look for ways to make new ideas work, not for reasons they won't.

5. We will speak positively about each other and about our organization at every opportunity.

6. We will communicate goals and activities within and between departments.

7. We will respect each other's time and priorities, be courteous in our interactions, and have a positive attitude.

8. We will actively engage and get to know our coworkers.

9. We will recognize and value each other's achievements and contributions, both large and small.

10. We will take pride in our facility and take initiative to help maintain a clean and safe environment for all.

11. We will...Have fun.

Photo credit Beck Center

In order to engage people who have been a part of the Beck Family, an alumni program was established. Alumni are those who have participated in LLT/Beck Center education and/or professional theater programs who want to stay connected. A Facebook page for Beck alumni was started, and an annual Holiday Homecoming Party was held for several years. Beck Center hosted an annual trip to New York City for ten consecutive years for supporters to see shows together and visit with Beck alumni on Broadway, until the pandemic forced a pause in 2020. Joe Rosenberg of VIP Tours of NYC, who hosted the annual excursions, continued to welcome Beck friends by producing an online version of the NYC experience, along with Scott Spence, in September, 2020.

2015-16 - *Mary Poppins* starring Rebecca Pitcher; Photo credit Kathy Sandham

Beck management staff began to understand and appreciate the art of "not trying to do everything" and "be everything" to the community. The business philosophy shifted in some key ways, including appreciating the concept of "hidden costs" that come with renting out areas of the facility for non-mission-related activity; and realizing that different skill sets and employees are needed to be a "producing organization" as opposed to a "presenting organization." Large investments in marketing and promotion are needed to present someone else's finished product playing in one of the theaters, and management staff learned to embrace the fact that producing theater, dance, and music performances utilizes local resources and talents. In the same vein of thinking, the conclusion was that Beck Center didn't have the resources or internal capacity to maintain an entire museum of paintings and sculptures.

An **_Art Collection Philosophy_** was adopted in 2015 under the leadership of then Associate Director of Visual Arts Darrelle Centuori:

> *Beck Center for the Arts will maintain a small but relevant art collection for the following reasons: to celebrate our commitment to visual art in a manner consistent to our mission of family inclusiveness, to provide aesthetic enjoyment and enrichment for staff and visitors alike, and to provide a resource for local art historians, now and in the future.*

> *In order to meet these standards of **commitment/mission consistency, aesthetics, and historical preservation,** Beck Center will ensure that our collection is well stored when necessary, well displayed, and well maintained through proper care and conservation.*

2016 - *In the Heights* - Beck Center/Baldwin Wallace University collaborative production
Photo credit Roger Mastroianni

Every few years, Beck Center Board of Directors undertakes a visioning process to update the organization's strategic plan. In 2012, a more aspirational future-oriented goals plan was completed, including a vision for an arts campus which would match the high quality of the programs. Strategies to grow our programs through increased visibility and access was a priority, as well as increasing the quality of work life for employees. A major re-branding initiative was completed, including an updated Beck logo and messaging.

2015 – Beck Center Board of Directors and management team; photo credit Beck Center
(L-R) Fred Unger, Larry Goodpaster, Joel Egertson, Scott Spence, Cindy Einhouse, Max Thomas, Adrienne Embery-Goode, Maggie Weitzel, Kathy Haber, Jenny Febbo, Kathleen McGorray, Tom Wagner, Doug Hoffman, John Reynolds, Ellen Todia, Mary Anne Crampton, Ed Gallagher, Kathy Caffrey, Richard Fox, Monica Brown, Brad Richmond MD

In 2015, the Board of Directors voted in support of moving forward with a capital campaign *Creating Our Future* to position the organization to be a national model of integrated arts education and performance. This capital campaign, set to begin in 2016, would be the largest comprehensive capital campaign in the history of the organization. Campaign Co-Chairs at the outset were Mary Kim Elkins and Douglas Hoffman.

With portions of buildings constructed over 100 years ago, the campus was in need of changes to accommodate individuals with mobility issues, wheelchair access, more convenient placement of public restrooms, and fewer steps which can impede patrons and students of any ages. Through fundraising for these improvements, Beck Center would have spaces that better reflect the quality of the education programs and the professional productions on the stages.

Priorities of the *Creating Our Future* campaign were to:
- Transform the main building and the old Armory into beautiful, inviting, accessible and energy efficient spaces for teaching, performance and community gathering,
- Build on the strength of the Dance program by creating a new, dedicated Center for Dance, and
- Create a Program Initiatives Launchpad (PIL), a Board directed fund under the guidance of the Board of Directors, for the purpose of investing in technology and program

initiatives for the future. Priority will be given to those initiatives which increase Beck Center's capability to connect with underserved populations and integrate emerging trends in arts performance and education into the programming, including online and virtual classes and events.

Before anyone else in the community was approached, each Board member was personally contacted and solicited, and within the next year, over $1,500,000 was received in total from 100% of the Board.

Design and construction partners included Bialosky and Turner Construction. Bialosky, a local architectural firm, designed the Edgewater Beach House, American Greetings World Headquarters, Pura Vida restaurant, and Crocker Park. Turner Construction's work can be seen at Playhouse Square and the Case Western Reserve University, Cleveland Clinic Health Education Campus. Douglas Hoffman represented Beck Center on the entire renovation project.

After Mary Kim Elkins left the Board, Sandra Sauder and Ellen Todia stepped in to Co-Chair the campaign with Douglas Hoffman. (Along with Ms. Einhouse, Development Director Dena Adler led the staff support until Ms. Adler left her position in 2021.)

2018-19 *Shrek* – photo credit Andy Dudik

2018 – *Hair* - Beck Center and Baldwin Wallace University Music Theatre collaboration
Photo credit Roger Mastroianni

"I am a corporate lawyer, very comfortable with analyzing legal issues and working to solve them. Painting involves 'that other half of my brain' that rarely got much exercise, so learning to paint and learning to love painting has been a wonderful and lasting addition to my life. [Our teacher] is capable of working with us at our own level and giving us the confidence to exceed our expectations."

— Pat Oliver: is an attorney with Tucker Ellis LLP, and has been a student of Beck Center's Watercolor class since 2008

Beck Center
—FOR THE arts—

Visual Arts Student: Photo credit Wetzler Studios

2019 – Kathryn Tokar[17] – photo credit Liz Knutsen for Charlottesville Ballet

---

[17] A former student of Melanie Szucs at Beck Center, Ms. Tokar has a degree in dance from Mercyhurst and began her professional career as a founding member of the new Cleveland Ballet. She spent a season performing as a company member with the Lake Erie Ballet, under the direction of Lesley Bories-Scalise, and as a guest artist at North Pointe Ballet, under the direction of Janet Strukely-Dziak. In 2017, she joined the Charlottesville Ballet (under the direction of Emily Hartka & Sara Clayborne) in Virginia. She was teaching and doing administrative work for Charlottesville Ballet through the pandemic, while also going back to school (online) to work on a Master's in Arts in

2019 *Dance Treasures in the Attic* – photo credit Kim Parrish

2021 – Riley Haley[18]; photo credit Christyl O'Flarhety

Medicine. As of December 2021, she was teaching in a Movement For Parkinson's program, after returning to live performance with Deos Contemporary Ballet in summer 2021 and then with Charlottesville Ballet in fall 2021.

[18] As of December 2021, Ms. Haley was a second-year student at University of California, Santa Barbara studying to earn a BFA in dance and a BS in Cell and Developmental Biology. A former student of Melanie Szucs at Beck Center, she has been selected as an apprentice for The Santa Barbara Dance Theater professional company. During the fall of 2021, she was selected to perform in the seniors' BFA choreography projects, Kinetic Lab.

Inspired by his childhood experiences with LLT, sculptor David Deming (retired President & CEO of the Cleveland Institute of Art) chose to make a gift of one of his works, and in November 2020, Beck Center's newest sculpture *Flora Bella* was installed near the front entrance.

November 2020 - David Deming and Lucinda Einhouse; photo credit Beck Center

"My experience with Beck Center has had a hugely positive effect on me. I watch or partake in the work that they do, and it is one of the rare times where hope isn't an abstract idea or ideal...it's an action or series of planning and action. The full possibilities of what Beck Center can be has not been tapped yet. That excites me."

— Martinez E-B: is a working artist based in Chicago, IL, who has shown his work in our gallery and participated in our outreach education programs

Beck Center
—FOR THE arts—

"I put Beck Center in a really different category, because while certain events have changed certain aspects of my life, I really think of my time at Beck Center as a completely transformative experience. The skills that I learned while being here and the confidence that it gave me has really transformed who I am today." Colin Moeller, attorney

CHAPTER 10:
Positioning for the Future – 2020+

Beck Center was experiencing a stellar year with record theater ticket sales, class registrations, and contributions, when everything came to a screeching halt in March 2020 with the arrival of the world-wide COVID-19 pandemic – one of the deadliest pandemics in the history of the world. This severe respiratory disease was transmitted through the air from those infected to others in close proximity. Those with the virus could spread it even if they did not have any symptoms. Millions of individuals experienced serious illness and/or death, especially the elderly, while others experienced very mild symptoms. The randomness and uncertainly led to a high degree of anxiety and fighting between political parties and communities of individuals.

Authorities worldwide responded by implementing travel restrictions, lockdowns and quarantines, workplace protocols, and business closures. Misinformation circulated through social media and mass media caused panic buying, food shortages, and inconsistent use of preventative measures such as social distancing, self-isolation for people exposed, and wearing face masks in public. Theaters and arts organizations all over the country closed their doors, and artists became the largest group of those unemployed.

It was a time of great uncertainty and stress, as no one knew how long the shutdown would go on, and hospitals became overwhelmed with patients needing intensive care for COVID-19. Members of minority groups suffered disproportionately to the rest.

The pandemic raised issues of racial discrimination and health equity, as well as the question of individual rights vs public health. Distrust of health officials by people of color, due to a history of abuse, caused many to refuse the vaccine, while at the same time, there existed a lack of access to resources and preventative care. (The availability of vaccines in the spring of 2021 allowed individuals to become more comfortable with engaging in public events once again.)

On top of this, racial tensions hit a breaking point when on May 25, 2020, George Floyd, a 46-year-old black man was killed in Minneapolis, Minnesota by a white police officer who was arresting him on suspicion of using a counterfeit $20 bill. While a crowd gathered and took pictures and videos for social media, the police officer knelt on Mr. Floyd's neck for over nine minutes after he was handcuffed and lying face down, and even after another officer took his pulse and found him to be deceased. The videos went viral, and Mr. Floyd's murder led to worldwide protests against police brutality and racism.

In Cleveland, Ohio, on May 30, 2020, a peaceful demonstration to protest the death of George Floyd, turned into violence and civil unrest. Police officers, Fire and EMS personnel were attacked by rioters as they responded to several locations. During this time frame, the number of individuals grew as people who were not originally part of the protest converged downtown.

Within a few hours, damage to businesses across the city became widespread. Several on Euclid Avenue were set on fire and had windows smashed. Cleveland Mayor Frank Jackson spoke with Ohio Governor Mike DeWine about bringing in the National Guard. Mayor Jackson signed an emergency proclamation mandating a curfew for the Central Business District and part of the Ohio City neighborhood. The city-wide curfew lasted for nearly a week, and many businesses in sympathy with the cause created public anti-racism statements, including Beck Center for the Arts.

For several weeks after, the Beck Center marquee featured the following statement: "We Stand Together For Change." This message was distributed to faculty, staff, Board members and volunteers from Lucinda Einhouse, President/CEO on June 1, 2020:

> *Dear Beck Center Family,*
>
> *I am reaching out today to "check in" during this difficult time. As we take our first small steps towards recovering from a global pandemic, the murders of Black citizens in our country and the violent disruption of peaceful and necessary protest throughout the United States has been heartbreaking.*
>
> *As employees, volunteers, patrons, and students, we must stand together to combat hate and promote justice. Systemic racism in our country is very real and those of us born into privileged positions must stand hand-in-hand with the Black community to say "enough is enough!"*
>
> *I am thankful we work for an organization that is invested in anti-racism – which means a commitment to examine and constantly improve our own values and practices. I am proud of our passion for diversity, accessibility, and inclusion. We hope to be a beacon for you, and to create an environment where you can feel safe, loved, and respected.*
>
> *Cindy Einhouse*

Foundation funders all over the country leaned on non-profit organizations to take the lead in addressing racial disparity in programming, staffing, and volunteer leadership, as a stipulation to receiving grants.

The Beck Family has always strived to be thoughtful, authentic, and strategic. This is especially important as the organization evolves toward being a multi-cultural organization. Beck Center's core values are at the heart of its mission: 1) Diversity as an essential component in all we do, and 2) An inclusive and safe environment. Like arts organizations all around the country, Beck Center's existence was threatened because of the pandemic and the limited ability to generate earned revenue, but was still committed to its mission to serve the community.

JOURNEY TO BELONGING

From October 2020- March 2021, Beck Center engaged Victor Ruiz and his firm Gradient Think Tank (Gradient) to facilitate a Board retreat titled "A Journey to Belonging." Consulting work with Gradient was paid for through Beck Center's operating budget. Key concepts: inclusiveness, culture of belonging, human equity. Immediately following that retreat, the Board created a new standing committee for Diversity, Equity, and Inclusion (DEI) under the guidance of Gradient, with Board member Co-Chairs Chann Fowler-Spellman and Angie Kazi. This DEI Committee works alongside the Governance Committee to guide the organization along its journey to belonging and anti-racism.

From March to July 2021, thanks to the support of the Char and Chuck Fowler Family Foundation, Beck Center was able to engage Gradient to continue DEI work of the Board; to develop a customized DEI strategic plan that results in measurable goals and outcomes, including a North Star Statement for both the Board and organization wide, collaborative input and buy-in, accountability, and long-term sustainability. Goals were drafted for the Board and for the faculty/staff. Significant support from The Nord Family Foundation was then received to fund the remainder of the work with Gradient. Aspirational vision statements were adopted by the Board, faculty, and staff:

> BOARD OF DIRECTORS "NORTH STAR"
> *The Beck Center Board welcomes and engages individuals who share the goal of enhancing the human spirit through arts experiences. We believe a diverse and inclusive Board will make just and valuable decisions. We lead by committing to continuous learning for deeper understanding of equity and inclusion, including racial and ethnic equity, and courageously using this understanding to improve upon all Board work and service.*

> ORGANIZATIONAL "NORTH STAR"
> *Beck Center for the Arts welcomes and engages every individual who shares the goal of enhancing the human spirit through arts experiences. We believe in the transforming and transcending power of the arts, the strength of collaboration, an inclusive and safe environment, and diversity as an essential component in all we do. We are committed to continuous learning for deeper understanding of equity and inclusion, using this understanding to create an environment that connects all people, communities, and cultures through the arts.*

Beck Center engaged Gradient Think Tank to work with the Board and leadership to develop a three-year strategic plan for growth and sustainability that fully integrates diversity, equity, and inclusion. Gradient worked with Beck leadership to ensure that the scope of work, timeline, actions required of staff, and deliverables were consistent with the expectations and aligned to the capabilities of all. Beck Center's staff who identify as BIPOC (Black, Indigenous, People of Color) took part in focus group discussions with Gradient.

RESPONDING TO THE PANDEMIC
After closing the Beck campus in March 2020, staff and faculty created free online arts programming (#BeckAtHome) within one week, crafted communications to hundreds of individuals cancelling performances, rehearsals, classes, and started working on pandemic safety protocols. Beck Center prepared for the 2020-2021 season not knowing what the environment would allow.

A spring 2020 mini-session offered 18 online classes that ran April 27 to June 6, including Kids-N-Tunes, ballet, cartooning, and acting on platforms like Zoom and/or Google Classroom. This was good preparation for the full semester schedule online in summer 2020. Music Therapy sessions were conducted in-person during summer 2020, after the initial state mandated lockdown was eased, which allowed for a decrease in students' anxiety and an increase in their ability to cope with the challenges they were facing during the pandemic.

When faced with an operating deficit for the fiscal year 2020-2021, Beck Center was forced to lay off or furlough several employees, and all of the remaining staff took a voluntary pay cut of 10%-20% as of August 2020.

When the 2020-2021 season began in September 2020, a number of in-person classes were provided (maximum of 9 students per class with 6-foot distancing and masks enforced) alongside the online offerings. However, in November due to the County advisory and alert regarding the high number of COVID cases, Beck Center was once again forced to close the campus and return to all online programming.

Beck Center's first ever video on-demand professional theater production *Fully Committed* opened November 13, 2020. While revenue for on-demand ticket sales was limited, production expense was relatively low, and feedback was overwhelmingly positive. Marketing a virtual production is like marketing any other new product or start-up; it takes more time and expense, and theater critics do not tend to write much about these virtual productions.

The online Youth Theater production of *Zopp* was a very positive experience for the students and audiences, including recognition from Northeast Ohio Parent Magazine. The Youth Theater matinee performances of *Zopp* and *A Christmas Peril* welcomed students from: Alliance City Schools, The Centers – Clifton Early Childhood Center, Cleveland Municipal School District, Fairview Park Schools, Lakewood City Schools, Lakewood Child Care, Our Lady of Angels, and Rocky River City Schools.

Youth Theater *Zopp* – online production November 2020; *photo credit Beck Center*

This was a time of high stress and anxiety for everyone. Board members expressed their appreciation of staff members by personally delivering to their homes hand-written thank you notes and gift boxes during December 2020.

During the Winter/Spring Semester beginning January of 2021, both in-person and online classes were offered, although the in-person classes registered many more students than the online experiences. People expressed a craving for safe, in-person experiences and trusted Beck Center to provide this.

In February 2021, *5x15: Five World Premiere 15-Minute Musicals,* an online production by Beck Center and Baldwin-Wallace University Music Theatre, marked the 10th year of this collaboration.

The Dance Department was able to successfully stream a beautiful video of *The Nutcracker* production March 12-14, 2021, which had unfortunately been postponed from November 2020 due to the shift back to all online activity.

Over the course of 2020-2021, staff leadership spent considerable time advocating for public relief funding for the arts at the national, state, county, and local levels. Members of the management team got

August 2021 – Summer Camp students with Assistant Technical Director Tim Chrisman

involved with numerous task forces and advocacy groups, communicating the devastating impact of the pandemic on the arts, while noting the economic impact and critical need for the arts in the lives of individuals, especially considering the dramatic increase in the problem of depression and isolation. When sufficient pandemic relief funding was received by the spring of 2021, the Board voted to restore the salaries and pay each staff member back what was cut.

Pandemic relief funds enabled Beck Center to continue its programming and retain talented faculty and staff during the 2020 pandemic year. Thanks to the submission and management of complex grant requests by Director of Finance and Operations Larry Goodpaster, Beck Center received Paycheck Protection Program (PPP) funding and a Shuttered Venue Operations Grant from the federal government, CARES Act funds from the State of Ohio through Ohio Arts Council and also from Cuyahoga County through Cuyahoga Arts & Culture (CAC). Gratitude goes to County Executive Armond Budish and County Councilman Dale Miller for allocating Federal relief funding to the arts through Cuyahoga County.

2021 - summer camp, visual arts; photo credit Beck Center

2021 – summer Day of Dance and parking lot show; photo credit Beck Center

In July 2021, Beck Center received permission to produce live theater once again, and thus was the first in the region to bring union actors back to the stage with the July production *This Girl Laughs, This Girl Cries, This Girl Does Nothing*, as it paved the way for opening the 2021-2022 season in September.

As more and more people became vaccinated, the number of people signing up for summer classes and camps at Beck Center continued to increase. By the beginning of summer 2021, enrollment was up substantially compared to this same time two years ago (pre-pandemic). And 95% of that enrollment was for in-person arts experiences, 5% online. The numbers of students in each class and camp were still limited in order to keep appropriate spacing, but more classes and camps were scheduled.

2020 - music lesson (#BeckAtHome) learning ukulele with Dr. Wooley;
Photo credit Syma Dar

2021 – Dance students distanced and masked; photo credit Beck Center

Keeping an eye on protocols of other theaters in the area, along with advice from health care professionals and local governing authorities, Beck Center maintained a mask mandate for classes and camps, since 70% of students were under the age of 12 and therefore unvaccinated. Effective July 2021, a mask mandate was implemented for patrons attending professional theater performances.

Beck Center participated in Piano Cleveland's Piano Scavenger Hunt as one of ten locations across the region. Richard Duarte Brown, whose art has been previously displayed in the gallery leading to the Studio Theater and in the Skylight Gallery, designed the piano art which was inspired by both music and his personal story.

A display box on top of the piano was created to house a Little Free Library which was nationally registered in 2021: https://littlefreelibrary.org/ focused on the arts. The public is welcome to contribute any dance, music, theater, visual arts, poetry or other arts related books of any type and for any ages and take what's there.

Director of Finance and Operations Larry Goodpaster led the installation of new ticketing software in time for Beck Center's first live production since the pandemic shut-down, in the summer of 2021. This was necessary because the previous ticketing system company went out of business due to the pandemic.

Led by Director of Education Ed Gallagher, Beck Center's Creative Arts Therapies Department began producing a video series to be shown on the closed-circuit TV of LSC Service Corporation's senior centers. Funded by the Three Arches Foundation, the programs include music and visual arts.

Beck Dance Faculty member Madi Jackson founded MadJax Dance Company in June 2020, an all-level dance company whose mission is to bring together performers interested in social activism and company members that lift up the world around them through philanthropy. Beck Center provided an outdoor venue for MadJax's performance on Juneteenth (June 19), 2021.

In preparation for the return to live performances, ionization units were installed in the Senney Theater, the lobby, and the Studio Theater to freshen the air flow in large gathering spaces.

2021 Lakewood Arts Festival painting by Richard Duarte Brown; photo credit Beck Center

CAPITAL CAMPAIGN AND RENOVATIONS IN THE MIDST OF THE PANDEMIC

With 50% of the *Creating Our Future* campaign goal achieved, Beck Center had kicked off the public phase of the campaign on March 10, 2020, right before the Governor began shelter-in-place orders due to the pandemic. The campaign team of volunteers had been enlarged to continue to raise funds toward this important effort, and Beck faculty and staff had to focus hard to keep the arts a part of people's lives with online programming. The Board of Directors faced a difficult decision, to go ahead with the campaign, or shut it down temporarily. The Board chose to not only move forward with the campaign but began renovations to the oldest part of Beck Center's campus in August 2020 – the original LLT structure.

The Education Wing façade – August 2020; photo credit Beck Center

It was a smart and bold choice of the Board and then Chair of the Board Douglas Hoffman, to begin the renovation project in August 2020, at a time of tremendous uncertainty around the country due to the pandemic. However, Beck Center was able to save time and money by undertaking this very messy and disruptive work while there were a limited number of people in the building, due to remote programming capability, and most of the staff working from home. Patricia Oliver took over as Chair of the Board in September 2020 when Mr. Hoffman's term ended, and she fully endorsed the Board's decision to move forward with the campaign and the renovations.

Education Wing facing east, pre-renovation 2020; photo credit Beck Center

Education Wing facing west, under renovation November 2020; photo credit Beck Center

Fowler-Spellman Education Wing facing east, March 2021; photo credit Beck Center

2021 completion of "pocket park" renovations and sculpture Flora Bella donated by Lakewood Little Theater alumnus and retired President, Cleveland Institute of Art, David Deming; photo credit Beck Center

Artistic Director Scott Spence did a series of short videos on site to keep everyone updated on the progress, and the Development Department team created communications along with Director of Marketing Julie Gilliland[19] to keep the public informed.

Beck Center was granted $300,000 through the State of Ohio's capital budget for the renovation project, thanks to the leadership of Senator Nickie Antonio and Representative Michael Skindell.

Renovation of the Education Wing was complex due to the age of the building (vintage 1915), but the team managed to complete the work by February 2021, under the guidance of Immediate Past Chair of the Board and Campaign Co-Chair Douglas Hoffman.

On March 10, 2021, Beck Center marked the achievement of a significant milestone - a ribbon cutting ceremony celebrating the completion of the first phase of the renovation project – the newly renovated Fowler-Spellman Education Wing. The celebration marked the one-year anniversary of the kick-off of the public phase of the campaign (March 2020), when attainment toward the goal was 50% (over $3,000,000). By March 2021, during the height of the pandemic, an additional $1,000,000 had been raised, which caused the Board to raise its sights and increase the goal of the campaign to $6,700,000.

A "Pocket Park" renovation was completed in March 2021 on the western side of Beck Center's front yard, thanks to a grant from Cuyahoga County, in partnership with the City of Lakewood. County Councilman Dale Miller was a key leader and advocate for Beck Center and the arts in Cuyahoga County. Board Member Jeff Poore oversaw the many details involved with that project.

Beck Center won first place in *Cleveland Magazine's* Best of the Best in April, 2021, a competition which involved 160 companies & non-profit organizations from Best of the West, Best of the East, and Best of Cleveland. This is a testament to Beck friends who voted and Beck Center's extremely effective marketing department and social media campaign.

---

[19] See APPENDIX A

Thanks to the work of Marketing Director Julie Gilliland and Associate Director of Theater Education Sarah Clare and others, Beck Center was featured in a WKYC commercial about "coming together to uplift the community."

In May 2021, the Beck Board voted to move forward with the next stage of renovations - the back building on campus, the former Armory, to create a Center for Music & Creative Arts Therapies. Work took place August 13, 2021 through mid-December, 2021, and a celebration of its completion was held on March 10, 2022.

August 2021 - Armory under renovation; photo credit Beck Center

January 2022 – renovated Recital Hall, in the Center for Music and Creative Arts Therapies

March 10, 2022 – MCAT Ribbon Cutting, (L-R): Board Chair Patricia Oliver, Lakewood Mayor Meghan George, County Councilman Dale Miller, Director of Education Edward Gallagher, President & CEO Lucinda Einhouse, State Senator Nickie Antonio, Capital Campaign Co-Chair Sandra Sauder, Capital Campaign Co-Chair Douglas Hoffman

The Capital Campaign Committee, led by Co-Chairs Doug Hoffman – Immediate Past Chair of the Board, Sandra Sauder and Ellen Todia, President & CEO Lucinda Einhouse, and Development Director Megan DeFranco[20] sought to raise the remainder of the $6,700,000 goal so the final segment of renovations could take place in 2022-2023: Building an ADA (Americans with Disabilities Act) accessible main entrance, a new marquee, restrooms near the front door, and finally raising the roof of the main building to accommodate two new state-of-the-art dance studios.

> *"From the inception of this capital campaign we compared the cost of new construction versus renovating our existing Beck buildings. We determined that renovation would bring our buildings up to industry standards at about 25% of the cost of a new building, excluding land cost if we chose to build in a new location. Additionally, we could continue to offer exciting programming even during the phased construction. Ironically, the pandemic provided a unique opportunity to undergo renovation when the buildings were essentially closed, saving time and expense. It was an exciting challenge to move forward during this difficult time, but our Beck Board wisely chose to proceed, and by the end of 2021 we will have over half our campus renovated."*
> (Douglas Hoffman, October, 2021)

---

[20] See APPENDIX A

The third phase of renovations also involved tearing down the "Annex Building" on the corner of Rockway and Detroit Avenues to create the eastern portion of Beck Center's front yard pocket park. The cost of renovating the annex building was estimated to be substantial, and its odd shape not ideal for programming. Demolishing it would provide much more visibility to the main building and open up the front driveway to less congestion.

Photo credit Beck Center

January 2022 plan for the east "Pocket Park" – DERU Landscape Architecture

RENAMING THE SENNEY THEATER

Decades ago, one of the buildings along the west end of Detroit Avenue in Lakewood next to the Lucier Movie Theatre bore the name Maheu across the brickwork. Wally Senney remembers riding his bike past the building as a kid and recognizing the name from his family tree.

That family connection is part of the reason Mr. Senney and his wife, Joyce, made a generous contribution to Beck Center's $6,700,000 *Creating Our Future* capital campaign. But their inspiration went beyond that. They felt very strongly that the non-profit, performing arts and arts education organization made Lakewood a better community. And that it deserved updated facilities to carry out its mission of inspiring, enriching and transforming lives in northeast Ohio through dynamic arts experiences.

"We think the Beck Center is quite a jewel that we have right here in Lakewood," Wally Senney said. *"It not only trains actors and people who end up on Broadway, but it's got classes for adults and students, whether it be in the arts, pottery, music or dance."*

Wally Senney's great-uncle Albert Maheu built the building that is now part of Beck Center's campus. Albert's nephew Arthur Maheu was Wally Senney's stepfather. Arthur's mother played piano during silent movies played at the old Lucier Motion Picture Theatre, which became the home of the Lakewood Little Theatre, where Wally Senney took an acting class as a child. All three of Wally and Joyce's children took arts classes at the theater, which by the mid-1970s had become known as Beck Center for the Arts. Theirs is just one of many generations of families who have experienced and benefited from Beck Center for the Arts.

"I really feel it will impact the community because the outside of it will be so visibly attractive that more people will drive by and say, 'Oh, my gosh, I didn't know this was here.' A lot of people think all they do is plays. That's one part of it, but there's 20 more parts of it. The dance program at Beck is very big. Kids come from all over, and we know a lot of people right here in our community that are part of it, too. It's great to see kids that we know using it and loving it and being a part of it." (Joyce Senney, 2021)

"It's all of our responsibility to try and leave the world a better place than we found it. The arts are a really good place for our dollars." (Wally Senney, 2021)

Beck Center's Spotlight gala on July 17, 2021 at the beautiful new Gordon Green venue in Cleveland's Gordon Square, themed "All the World's a Stage," highlighted the legacy program of the organization - theater. During the pandemic, it had become especially evident that live performances had been greatly missed, and people need theater in their lives to invoke thoughts and feelings through experience and observation. Honorees of Spotlight 2021 were Wally and Joyce Senney, lead donors to the *Creating Our Future* capital campaign, and Artistic Director Scott Spence, recognizing his 30th season at Beck Center. With 250 people attending, the celebration raised valuable dollars toward the Center's arts and education programming.

July, 2021 – Celebrating Artistic Director Scott Spence's 30th season
(L-R)Scott Spence, Senator Nickie Antonio, Joyce Senney; Photo credit Steve Wagner

Beck Center for the Arts "Spotlight Gala"

Chuck and Char Fowler with Chris Kascsak and Bret Manning

Scott, Rachel and Carleigh Spence with Donnie Grimm

Beck Center for the Arts' Spotlight Gala celebrated 88 years of its professional theater program in the event space Gordon Green in Gordon Square.

The evening's 255 guests honored major donors Wally and Joyce Senney and Artistic Director Scott Spence. The Senneys are longtime donors and fans of Beck Center's theater program. They also have a long history at Beck Center beginning with Lakewood Little Theater.

"Joyce and I have been residents of Lakewood for most of our lives. Along with our family who all still live in Lakewood, we want to do whatever we can to not only keep Lakewood a great place to live, but also improve it. The Beck Center is a jewel that brings many people, young and old, into our community to learn and study the arts and sends them out with confidence, talents and skills that end up putting some on Broadway," Wally Senney said. "We want our name on the Senney Theater to keep us identified as part of Lakewood and also because our family once owned the original theater that is part of the Beck campus."

Scott Spence, artistic director for more than 30 years, has directed and produced more than 100 titles at Beck Center. "I'm thrilled to celebrate this milestone with my extended Beck family," he said. "To have a home to create for 30 years is really as good as it gets for an artist. I wake up every day more grateful than the day before."

Lucinda Einhouse, Beck Center president and CEO noted, "After such an extended intermission, it feels good

Joyce and Wally Senney

to be getting together in person and celebrating theater, especially since this is the legacy program of Beck Center. I'm grateful for the opportunity to put the spotlight on Scott whose talent has shown on our stages for so many decades. And I'm especially grateful to put the spotlight on Wally and Joyce whose exceptional philanthropic gift is a statement of their commitment to the future of this historic organization."

Mike O'Brien, a Beck Center board member added, "Beck enhances the human spirit of the people it serves. Beck makes people better."

Spotlight included entertainment by artists recreating their original vocal performances from various musicals directed by Scott Spence. Traci Nolan served as Spotlight chair. Bill Litzler returned as the evening's emcee. Dinner was prepared by Chef Chris Hodgson of Driftwood Catering.

The $140,000 in proceeds from Spotlight will advance Beck Center's mission to provide the community with arts education, performances, exhibitions, art therapies and an outreach program while creating art experiences for people of all ages and abilities. STORY BY CYNTHIA SCHUSTER EAKIN/PHOTOGRAPHS BY ERIC EAKIN

Mike and Molly O'Brien, Grant and Colleen Flennoy and Bridget O'Brien

Jack Brunner and Sandy Sauder with Lucinda and Tom Einhouse

Photo courtesy of Currents - Joyce and Wally Senney and Scott Spence, Honorees Spotlight Gala, July 2021

Moving forward, it will be the challenge of Beck Center's leadership to continue honoring the past while also recognizing those who contribute to the future. The organization's constant evolution is key to remaining dynamic, so that it will remain strong for future generations to enjoy.

As of 2022, some of Ken Beck's paintings remain prominently displayed in the main building, as pictured below. This is a reminder to all about a person who took up painting later in life and discovered a commitment to the arts. One person who, along with a dynamic team of individuals, took a bold step in the mid-1970s, at a time of a national economic crisis, to invest in the future of arts education and performances.

Ken Beck painting – photo credit Beck Center

Ken Beck painting – photo credit Beck Center

Ken Beck painting – photo credit Beck Center

2017 – Rory O'Malley as King George in *Hamilton,* backstage at the Pantages in Los Angeles
Photo credit Rory O'Malley

Not every student will become acclaimed in their field like Cleveland native and Tony Award Nominee Rory O'Malley, who embraced his love of theater through the Youth Theater program at Beck Center and is now an acclaimed professional actor. But every person deserves the opportunity to experience the transforming and transcending power of the arts.

The History of Beck Center for the Arts is still in the making.

CHAPTER 11:

Saluting Our Volunteers

Throughout the years, Beck Center has had many volunteer support groups, including the Women's Board, Men's Board, Drama Production Wing, Theater Alliance of Beck Center (TABC), Dance Alliance of Beck Center (DABC), Action Community of Teen Theater (ACTT) - a group of theater students performing service projects, Connect to Beck – a young professionals support group whose name later changed to the Associate Board, as well as individual volunteers who served as ushers, landscapers, concession workers, and as backstage support for productions. Since 2008, members of the Lakewood/Rocky River Rotary have volunteered two mornings every year, spring and fall, to help maintain the landscaping. The following is a summary of work which cannot do justice to the depth of commitment and philanthropic involvement of these volunteers, but is an attempt to humbly and sincerely acknowledge their love and devotion to the organization.

Associate Board:
The Associate Board's mission is to raise the awareness of Beck Center, increase the involvement of young professionals in the organization and our community, and raise needed funds for the organization. For many years, the Associate Board assisted the staff with producing the "Bike for Beck" fundraising event, as well as introduction of new audiences to Beck Center through their "Taste and Create" events, with themes like "Beer and Improv."

Dance Alliance of Beck Center (DABC):
DABC was founded to support the general program of the dance department at Beck Center and underwrites much of the cost of costumes for the dance workshop performers as well as providing scholarship assistance for special dance instruction programs and events. DABC was formalized as a volunteer organization in 2002 with Carol Culp as President, however for many years before that, there were parents of children enrolled in dance classes who assisted faculty members in order to make their children's experience the best it could be. Members include not only parents, but grandparents, alumni, friends, and people who just love dance. Fundraising is done in an effort to keep the cost of classes and performances as affordable as possible. The group provides additional educational experiences through sponsoring master classes, and awarding yearly scholarships. They have also contributed to funding equipment, costumes, lighting, storage organization, meals during performances, and a new dance floor. Funds are raised through dues, honorariums paid for performances of the Dance Workshop, selling Beck Dance shirts/sweats, and dance performance contributions. They have paid for stereo systems, costumes for the Dance Workshop, flooring, dance barres, and other items through the years. They have held garage/rummage sales and facilitated many bake sales at Beck. In 2004, the Nutcracker High Tea (a biennial project) was instituted as the principal fundraising event of DABC.

Theater Alliance of Beck Center (TABC):
Involvement of parents of theater students goes back to the time of the founding of the program in 1948, when the group was known as the Educational Theatre Board (ETB). The name was later changed (possibly in the 1990s) to C.A.S.T. (The Company of Advocates for Students in Theater) and then to TABC (Theater Alliance of Beck Center) in 2011. TABC is comprised of families and friends of students enrolled in Theater Education courses and/or who perform in the Youth Theater productions at Beck Center. TABC's primary responsibilities are: 1) To support and enrich the student education experience; 2) Act as a liaison between families and

the Theater Education Staff; and 3) Provide crucial hands-on support to Youth Theater productions and events throughout the season. TABC raises funds through membership fees and performance souvenir sales which enables TABC to offer additional educational opportunities like master classes; fund the pit orchestra for the spring musical, host last day of semester receptions, purchase new equipment for the Theater Education department, and explore new ways to support Beck Center goals and improve the Youth Theater experience.

2014-2015 Youth Theater – Chicago; photo credit Wetzler Studios

Men's Advisory Board:
The Men's Advisory Board began as a volunteer arm of the Lakewood Little Theatre in 1937, devoted to supporting the work of the organization. The first meeting was held on October 21, 1937 at the home of Frederick Elder who became the first Chairman of the Men's Advisory Board. During the 1960s, in addition to being a working group, the Men's Advisory Board held regular meetings for members featuring speakers associated with the arts. In an announcement of their 1965-66 season, Mr. Sidney Adorn was promoted as a speaker for the group: *"He has some definitive thoughts about community theater. You may not agree with him but you won't be bored and you'll get a chance to argue with him."* Over the years, many projects geared to the upkeep of the building were funded and maintained by these members. When the 1976 building project became a reality, special projects were being completed by paid contractors. Membership dwindled over the following years, and in 2004 the Men's Advisory Board disbanded. As their final act, they donated $3,232 to pay for the cost of a new light board for the Studio Theater.

Drama Production Wing:
The Drama Production Wing (DPW) was established in 1948 "to aid in the promotion and welfare of The Lakewood Little Theatre, through the creation of interest in work pertaining to actual theater operation. DPW members were expected to participate in at least one regular theater production each season through any one of the following: acting, book-holding, checkroom, costuming, lighting, properties, ushering, clerical, house management, stage management, set construction, sound, set décor, and other scheduled activities.

As the theater productions had become more professionalized, members decided to limit their activities to helping to organize opening night receptions, pay for coffee during rehearsals and productions and organize an occasional social event for members. Minutes of a DPW general meeting on May 12, 1997 indicate that DPW President Shirley Toeller had spoken to Managing Director David Pierce about their deliberation as to whether or not the group should continue, and they decided to dissolve the group after the 1997-98 season.

Beck Center's Women's Board:
The Women's Board is Beck Center's longest standing volunteer group, established in 1936 as the Women's Committee. As of 2022, the Women's Board has contributed over $260,000 to Beck Center, over $50,000 to the *Creating Our Future* capital campaign, as well as thousands of volunteer hours.

Since the beginning, the Women's Board has been a fundraising and social membership group actively involved in furthering the mission of the organization. One of its first actions in 1936 was to encourage LLT to purchase the Lucier Motion Picture Theatre on Detroit and Wayne Avenues.

For many years, the Women's Board hosted opening night receptions for patrons and cast members of all of the theatrical productions. They also ushered and managed the usher crew. Bake sales, rummage sales, card parties, boutique sales, and luncheons were regular events. On the night of

2005 – Women's Board meeting in the Skylight Room; photo credit Cynthia Fisher

the final performance of a production, the Women's Board would feed those members of the cast and crew who stayed for "Strike Night" (disassembling and removing the set from the stage). If a show was scheduled for a double performance during a run, the Women's Board would feed cast and crew between the matinee and evening performances.

Following the construction of the main building in 1976, the Women's Board maintained the garden within the new gallery, as the Women's Board Museum Garden. In 1990-1991, they reported that the monthly maintenance cost was $75/month, and there was additional cost for the garden to be replanted every year. They tried hard to keep the garden alive for many years, however there was not enough light through the skylight roof to keep it maintained without a large cost.

As of 2022, the group hosts monthly lunch meetings from September through May, sponsors two annual fundraising events, and operates additional fundraising activities throughout the year, including an annual Victorian Tea. During the pandemic, these activities had to pause,

however members learned how to use the Zoom virtual meeting software and continued to gather monthly.

Quote from Marjorie Wiese in 2008 (now deceased):

"I joined the Women's Board in the early 1960's after being involved with the Children's Theater since 1955. In 1968, I was elected President of Women's Board. Over the years, we had many events to raise money for the Beck Center. In the 1960s and 70s, we had a yearly rummage sale. These events were

2005 – Lee Mackey and Georgia Burley; photo credit Cynthia Fisher

always a lot of hard work but also a lot of fun. We now have two money making events each year. Everyone pitches in on the events. For example, I have bought many plants for table decorations over the years for our October card party. As a member of the Women's Board, I have worked on many wonderful projects and also made many close friends over the years."

2006 – Carla Kowalski and Cynthia Fisher; photo credit Cynthia Fisher

Chapter 12: Appendices

APPENDIX A - 2022 MANAGEMENT AND PROGRAM LEADERS

LUCINDA (CINDY) EINHOUSE, President and CEO

A lifelong passion for the arts and commitment to the Greater Cleveland community has culminated in Cindy Einhouse's current role as President & CEO of Beck Center for the Arts. Since May 2007, she has worked closely with staff and Board of Directors to stabilize the organization's finances and increase its visibility and engagement with the community. From 2007 to 2022, the number of people served by Beck Center has grown 30% to over 60,000 across five counties, with a $6,700,000 capital campaign underway as of 2022.

Her educational background includes an MBA from Cleveland State University and a BA in Music from Kent State University. She began her career at Playhouse Square Foundation in 1980, building an annual fund program and assisting with a capital campaign to raise $37.7 million to renovate the historic Playhouse Square theatres. In 1995, she was recruited to the Cleveland Clinic as part of a management team to conduct a $225 million capital campaign, which concluded ahead of schedule in 2000. In 2001, she was recruited to the Cleveland Institute of Music (CIM) to direct a capital campaign to raise $40 million for facility expansion and endowment, successfully completed in September 2006.

Ms. Einhouse was a member of the Board and Executive Committee of LakewoodAlive from 2013-2020, a non-profit economic development organization. She served on the Board of the Lakewood Chamber of Commerce from 2008-2015 and was Chair of that Board from 2013 to 2015. She has served as a Mentor for Cleveland State University's Graduate student program and the Mandel Center for Nonprofit Organizations. She is a co-founder of the North Coast Women's Sailing Association, and she co-chaired the Arts Outreach Committee for the Gay Games 2014 in Cleveland. She was a volunteer tutor for Refugee Response 2018-2020, a mentor for College Now since 2019, and a volunteer for Cleveland Rape Crisis' Sing Out Chorus since 2000.

MEGAN DEFRANCO, Director of Development

Megan DeFranco joined Beck Center in September 2021 as Director of Development. Previously, Ms. DeFranco worked in the non-profit sector as the Director of Development for the YMCA of Greater Rochester in New York since 2008. Youth development, education and community outreach are personally important to her, and she is thrilled to join Beck Center. She has over 15 years of comprehensive fundraising experience with annual, capital, legacy, and grant writing experience. She led a Young Women of Color Initiative for the Rochester YMCA branch Boards and coordinated a community conversation, "90 Feet Under, What Poverty Does to People." She is a volunteer of the Alumni Association of Rochester Institute of Technology and a member of the Association of Fundraising Professionals. In preparation for her move to Cleveland, Ms. DeFranco participated in the Civic Leadership Institute at the Cleveland Leadership Center. She has also joined the Advisory Board of the Parker Hannifin Downtown YMCA in Cleveland, Ohio.

EDWARD GALLAGHER, MT-BC, Director of Education

Edward Gallagher, MT-BC received his Bachelor of Music in Music Therapy from the Cleveland Music Therapy Consortium and Cleveland State University. Mr. Gallagher oversees the area's most comprehensive arts education program with classes in dance, music, theater, and visual arts; creative arts therapies; and education outreach. He was the founder of the Creative Arts Therapies program at Beck Center, which was the first community-based program in Ohio. Prior to Beck Center, Mr. Gallagher founded a Creative Arts Therapies program in 1994 as the Director of Music Therapy at Riverside Academy of Music. Riverside merged with Beck Center in 2001.

Mr. Gallagher holds a graduate certificate in nonprofit management from the University of North Carolina at Greensboro. He is co-chair of the Ohio Music Therapy Task Force and has been appointed to serve on the Ohio Arts Council's Artists with Disabilities Access Program and is on the Advisory Committee for the West Shore Career-Technical District Theatre Arts program. He is Past President of the Cleveland Arts Education Consortium as well as the Great Lakes Region of the American Music Therapy Association (GLR-AMTA) and the Association of Ohio Music Therapists (AOMT). He has received the GLR-AMTA Service Award, the AOMT Past President's Award, and has been inducted into the Ohio State Fair Hall of Fame. He has been recognized by the City of Lakewood for bringing the healing power of music to the community. He is also Director of Operations for the All-Ohio State Fair Band and Youth Choir, two organizations featuring the talents of 400 high school instrumentalists and vocalists from throughout the state.

LARRY GOODPASTER, Director of Finance and Operations

Larry Goodpaster began at Beck Center in January of 1998 as Musical Director for the theater. Following two years volunteering (2008-2009) as a business process and software consultant, he was hired as Director of Business Operations in 2009. Mr. Goodpaster is currently the Director of Finance and Operations. His expanded role allows him to focus his extensive experience in finance and operations towards developing strategies to increase both contributed and earned revenue while overseeing Beck Center's operations. Goodpaster brings a wealth of business experience from his time as Assistant Dean for the Weatherhead School of Management at Case Western Reserve University and as a regional director for Kaplan Educational Services.

JULIE GILLILAND, Director of Marketing

Julie Gilliland came to the position of director of marketing at Beck Center in September 2018, following a myriad of historical events during her tenure with Cleveland Play House. She began her ten years in the "old building" at 85th & Euclid Avenue, worked through the move to downtown Cleveland's Theater District and the renovated Allen Theatre, Outcalt Theatre, and The Helen. She was part of the team when The Cleveland Play House received the 2015 Tony Award ® and celebrated the first Centennial Season of a professional regional theater company in the United States. Prior to that, she spent two years with The Cleveland Orchestra marketing and selling the Severance and Blossom seasons, after three years with Playhouse Square. Prior to moving to Cleveland she worked for nine years with the Denver Center for the Performing Arts, on the resident theatre company side of Denver Center Theatre Company as well as on the Broadway touring arm, Denver Center Attractions. Born and raised in Texas, she received a theatre degree from Texas Woman's University. She is a member of the Cleveland Bridge Builders' Class of 2013.

SCOTT SPENCE, Artistic Director

Scott Spence began his career at the Beck Center for the Arts in 1990 as the Associate Artistic Director and became the Artistic Director in 1992. Mr. Spence holds a BA in Theatre from the University of Nebraska and a Master of Fine Arts degree in Directing from Western Illinois University. He has also held adjunct faculty positions at Cuyahoga Community College in Cleveland, Baldwin Wallace University in Berea, and taught the Directing curriculum at Cleveland State University from 2010 to 2015. He is the recipient of the 2006 Northern Ohio Live Award for Theatre Achievement. In 2015, he was awarded the Key to the City by Lakewood Mayor Michael Summers, recognizing Mr. Spence's 25th season as Beck Center's Artistic Director. Matilda the Musical, in summer 2019, marked the 100th production he has directed at Beck Center.

TRACY AMMON, Associate Director of Creative Arts Therapies

Tracy holds a Bachelor of Music in Music Therapy from Baldwin-Wallace University and has been with the Beck Center in various roles and capacities since 2008. In addition to overseeing the Creative Arts Therapies department, she teaches several classes and provides services to individuals at Beck, as well as representing the department in the community by providing music therapy, adapted music, and early childhood developmental programming. Her philosophy is grounded not only in behaviorally based theology but also the premise that the arts belong to us all. She has always loved the emphasis Beck Center places on bringing the arts to the community and immersing itself in the people it represents.

SARAH CLARE, Associate Director of Theater Education

Sarah has a Bachelor's degree in Dramatic Arts from Cleveland State University with an emphasis on performance and directing. In addition she has a Resident Educator Summative Assessment (RESA) teaching license in Integrated Language Arts for grades 7-12. In addition to her role at Beck Center for the Arts, Sarah has been the resident choreographer and co-director for Rocky River Middle School's spring musical. She has worked throughout the Cleveland area as a performer, director, choreographer, costumer, and teacher.

Jessica F. McGrath, Assistant Director of Education overseeing Music Education and Visual Arts

Jessica is an arts administrator and violinist passionate about education and increasing access to the arts for all. She holds a Bachelor of Music in Violin Performance from Baldwin Wallace University and a Master of Science in Arts Administration from Boston University. As an administrator, Jessica has a background in Development & Fundraising, holding positions at Rainey Institute in Cleveland and Powers Music School in the Boston area. Jessica has been teaching violin since 2009, and has also taught through the Suzuki Program at Baldwin Wallace Community Music School in addition to Beck Center. Jessica has completed substantial Suzuki violin teacher training and has attended Mimi Zweig's teacher training workshop at Jacob's School of Music. She is an active member of the American String Teachers Association and the Suzuki Association of the Americas.

Melanie Szucs, Associate Director of Dance Education

Melanie Szucs, an instructor in jazz and ballet, joined the Dance Department faculty in 1984 and became Associate Director in 2007. Ms. Szucs leads Beck Center's largest education program, offering 80 classes weekly with over 600 dancers actively enrolled. She also serves as the director and choreographer of Beck Center Dance Workshop. She has choreographed dozens of dance productions, showcases and recitals. Her students have gone on to dance professionally, become dance educators, work in the arts, and to have a lifelong appreciation and love for the art of dance. In her early years, she was named Miss Dance Michigan and performed as a soloist with Dance Detroit. She studied with George Zorich and was on full scholarship with the School of Cleveland Ballet.

APPENDIX B - BECK CENTER PAST BOARD PRESIDENTS/CHAIRS

1938-1939	William A. Kurz
1939-1942	John N. Traxler
1943-1944	Lloyd R. Taylor
1944-1946	Gilbert H. Knight
1947-1948	Frederick W. Dorn
1949-1955	Frank E. Chesney
1956-1957	Lloyd R. Taylor
1957-1959	Mrs. Meldrum Berkey
1959-1965	Carl Stahley
1965-1977	Howard E. Egert
1977-1979	Quigg Lohr
1980-1990	Dr. Joseph H. Albrecht
1991-1994	Rosemary Corcoran
1994-1997	Leroy Parks
1998-1999	John Jefferson
1999-2000	Henry Holtkamp
2001-2005	Ron Waldheger
2005-2006	Rosemary Corcoran

*2006 Title changed from President of the Board to Chair

2006-2010	Frederick B. Unger*
2011-2013	Mary Kim Elkins
2014-2017	Margaret Weitzel
2017-2020	Douglas Hoffman
2020-2023	M. Patricia Oliver

APPENDIX C - PAST ARTISTIC, MANAGING, AND EXECUTIVE DIRECTORS

1931-1942	Richard Kay, General Manager
1946-1949	Gordon Klein, director
1949-1952	Bramer Carlson, director
1952-1953	Clay Franklin, director
1953-1954	Betty Piper, executive producer
1954-1986	Karl A Mackey, artistic and managing director
1986-1988	Fred Sternfeld, artistic director
1988-1990	no artistic director
1990-1992	William Roudebush, artistic director
1990-1992	Scott Spence, associate artistic director
1992-current as of 2022	Scott Spence, artistic director
1986-1991	Faith Killius, managing director
1991-1993	Andrea Krist, managing director
1993-1994	Team management under Rosemary Corcoran, president of the Board
1995-1998	David Pierce, managing director
1998-1999	Lisa Nespeca, managing director
2000-2003	Bill Beckenbach, managing director
2003-2005	Elizabeth Horrigan, executive director
2005-2007	Jim Walton, consultant, then interim executive director
2007-current as of 2022	Lucinda Einhouse, president & CEO

APPENDIX D - Women's Committee/Board Presidents

1936-39	Mrs. Carl F. Knirk (Olive)
1939-41	Mrs. Frederick L. Elder (Florence)
1941-42	Mrs. Hubert Lehr (Rita)
1942-44	Mrs. Otis Nolan (Bess)
1944-46	Mrs. Robert H. Seibert (Clarice)
1946-48	Mrs. Meldrum W. Berkey (Erna)
1948-50	Mrs. J. Browning Jones (Dorothy)
1950-51	Mrs. A.R. Virgien (Milli)
1951-53	Mrs. Howard H. Egert (Margaret)
1953-54	Mrs. Howard H. Hoffman (Vi)
1954-55	Mrs. Robert Elliott (Janet)
1955-56	Mrs. Richard P. Overmyer (Verle-Marie)
1956-57	Mrs. Walter Becker (Mabel)
1957-58	Mrs. John Conrad (Jean)
1958-60	Mrs. Norman J. Reiff (Virginia)
1960-62	Mrs. Frank A. Norcross (Janice)
1962-63	Mrs. Arnold Roterus (Harriet)

[Name of Women's Committee changed to Women's Board of LLT in 1963]

1963-64	Mrs. James Clegg (Dorothy)
1964-66	Mrs. George Emde (Gladys)
1966-68	Mrs. Charles A. Purdom (Gladys)
1968-70	Mrs. William L. Wiese (Marjorie)
1970-72	Mrs. Fred Kohler
1972-74	Mrs. Aubrey Milnes (Joyce)
1974-76	Mrs. Edward T. Scanlon (Helen)
1976-78	Mrs. Dorothy Behl
1978-80	Mrs. Lorna Hart
1980-82	Mrs. Paul Harper
1982-84	Mrs. Ed Molsio
1984-86	Mrs. H. Zimmerman
1986-87	Mrs. J. Prescott Benhan
1987-90	Marilla Marr
1990-93	Blanche Kappenhagen
1993-95	Helen Corns
1995-2011	Mrs. Richard Fisher (Cynthia)
2011-2013	Jan Brundage
2013-2015	Janice Mastin-Kamps
2015-current as of 2022	Marianne Monihan

APPENDIX E – NATIONAL BOARD and ALUMNI HALL OF FAME

National Board
Beck Center's National Board began in 1991 when President of the Board, Rosemary Corcoran, in an effort to bring visibility to the organization, led the initiative to recognize those who have achieved national prominence in their careers. Some had prior connection to Beck Center and some of those connections were cultivated.

So far, our National Board includes those in the field of theater since that is our legacy program, but we seek to also connect with and recognize those in the fields of dance, music, visual arts, and creative arts.

National Directors as of 2022:
- **Martin Savidge:** (CNN news correspondent) - a Beck Theater alumnus who served as Master of Ceremonies for the 75th Anniversary Benefit

- **Alice Ripley:** (Actor, singer, songwriter, and mixed media artist known for her various roles on Broadway in musicals, including the Pulitzer Prize-winning *Next to Normal*) - an alumna of our theater education program. 2009 Tony for Best Performance by a Leading Actress, *Next to Normal.*

Past National Directors (deceased):
- **Marge Redmond** (deceased 2020): Actor best known for her role as Sister Jacqueline in *The Flying Nun*). She grew up in Lakewood and performed on The Lakewood Little Theatre stage as a young girl.

- **Jack Riley** (deceased 2016): An American comedic character actor known for playing Elliot Carlin in *The Bob Newhart Show* and voicing Stu Pickles in *Rugrats*). Performed a gratis benefit concert for Beck Center in 1998.

- **Jack Lee** (deceased 2016): One of Broadway's leading conductors and musical directors. Jack was born in Lakewood, Ohio. He studied piano, singing and drama at the Baldwin Wallace Conservatory of Music. He worked as an actor in many productions at Cleveland Play House and Cain Park Theatre and was cast in the role of "Doc" on the CBS soap opera *Love of Life*. He accompanied Dee Hoty for a benefit concert for Beck Center and also performed with Rebecca Pitcher at Beck Center's 75th Anniversary Benefit.

ALUMNI HALL OF FAME
Inducted 2018 – Beck Center's 85th Anniversary celebration
    Rory O'Malley, Tony Nominee
    Matthew Rego, The Araca Group[21] (Broadway producers)
    Michael Rego, The Araca Group
    Hank Unger, The Araca Group

---

[21] The Araca Group – Founded in 1997 by partners Matthew Rego, Michael Rego, and Hank Unger, The Araca Group produces and merchandises live entertainment and theatrical events on Broadway and around the world. (araca.com)

APPENDIX F - SPOTLIGHT GALA HONOREES

The Spotlight Gala was initiated for the 80th anniversary of Beck Center in 2013. During the previous five years, Beck Center held a Mayor's Ball, initiated by Lakewood's Mayor Ed FitzGerald in 2008, 2009, 2010 and continued by Mayor Michael Summers in 2011 and 2012.

2013   Terry Stewart, President, Rock & Roll Hall of Fame, collaborative partner with Beck Center since 1999, "Toddler Rock"

2014   Paul Clark and PNC, corporate philanthropic leader

2015   Tom Fraser and First Federal Lakewood, corporate philanthropic leader

2016   David Dombrowiak, Community West Foundation, Creative Arts Therapies philanthropic leader

2017   Cecilia Render, Executive Director of the Nordson Corporation Foundation, arts education philanthropic leader

2018   Rosemary Corcoran, Past Board President and longest time Board member (1987-current as of 2022)
        Iris November, youth theater education philanthropic leader

2019   Betty Kemper, dance program philanthropic leader
        Lynda Sackett, founder of dance program and longest time employee (56 years: 1962-2019)
        Melanie Szucs, dance faculty member at Beck Center since 1984 and Associate Director of Dance Education, 2007-present

2020   Postponed due to pandemic

2021   Wally and Joyce Senney, capital campaign philanthropic leaders
        Artistic Director Scott Spence, 30th season

2022   The Gund Foundation, philanthropic leader

APPENDIX G - VOLUNTEER APPRECIATION AWARDS

In 2010, Beck Center began a new program to recognize and honor volunteers. All volunteers were invited to a pre-show reception and theater production, and one person was given the spotlight as "Volunteer of the Year."

Beginning in 2017, instead of "Volunteer of the Year," three awards were provided:

Leading Role Award
Awarded for distinguished leadership. A true "Ambassador" who makes a significant contribution to Beck Center.

Shining Star Youth Award
Awarded to a dedicated youth volunteer who gives a significant amount of time and energy to Beck Center.

Behind the Scenes Award
For the "unsung hero". The enthusiastic supporter, a volunteer who is committed to getting the job done at Beck Center.

In 2020 and 2021, the volunteer recognition event and awards were paused due to the pandemic.

"Behind the Scenes Award"
2019	William Schmitt	Honorary Board, Retired Eaton Employees leader
2018	Kate Mott	Women's Board
2017	Ruth Anne Havasi	Women's Board, Dance Alliance, usher & concessions

"Shining Star Youth Award"
2019	Audrey Carson	Youth Theater
2018	Kailee Shaver	Theater Education
2017	Megan Gallagher	Dance Department, Creative Arts ("Razzle Dazzle")
	Maggie Schneider	Dance Department, Creative Arts ("Razzle Dazzle")

"Leading Role Award"
2019	Doug Hoffman	Board, Capital Campaign Co-Chair and Project Manager
2018	Carrie Brindza	President, Dance Alliance (DABC)
2017	Mary Gagen	Past President, Dance Alliance (DABC), Spotlight Gala

"Volunteer of the Year"
2016	Jenniver Sparano	Costume Designer
2015	Katie Kurtz	Associate Board
2014	Karen Langenwalter	Business Analysis and Administration
2013	Don Carlson	Board of Directors, Finance
	Mary Kahelin	Professional Theater
2012	Theresa Burke	Theater Alliance of Beck Center (TABC)
	Ruth Bertrand	Board of Directors and Women's Board
2011	Carol Culp	Dance Alliance
2010	Georgia Burley	Women's Board

APPENDIX H - A Timeline - Lakewood Little Theatre and Beck Center for the Arts

1914   Bertrum C. Maheu was hired by Lambert Lucier to build the Lucier Motion Picture Theatre at 17823 Detroit Avenue

1931   Formation of "The Guild of the Masques," Managing Director Richard Kay, first production, Robert Sherwood's "The Queen's Husband" at West Side Evangelical church (38th and Bridge, Cleveland Ohio)

1933   Group incorporates into Lakewood Little Theatre (LLT) and performs at Gormson's Hall (18517 Detroit Avenue)

The Articles of Incorporation are dated May 16, 1933, signed by Gladys Rose, Lee Helm, Robert Seibert, Richard Kay, and William Kurz

1934   Opening of the Dramatic School of the Lakewood Little Theatre for adult members of LLT (18515 Detroit Avenue)

1936   Women's Committee organized (later called Women's Board), Olive Knirk as president

The Lucier Theatre was leased with an option to purchase

1937   Men's Advisory Board organized

Classes began in voice, diction, pantomime, and scenic design, in addition to a class in The Art of Play Production with instruction by Richard Kay

1938   Renovation of the Lucier for LLT was completed at a cost of $12,000, including a lighting system for $1,800, new stage and dressing rooms. 15 rows of seats were removed leaving a total of 465 seats

Drama classes began for children and adults

LLT's first production in Lucier Motion Picture Theatre; May 7, 1938, "Ladies of the Jury"

May 7-14, 1938 "Lakewood Little Theatre Week" – Mayor Amos I Kaufman proclamation

1939   Lakewood School of the Theater incorporation was completed, following the filing of the Articles of Incorporation in October of 1938.

1940   Took over store east of the lobby for use as a lounge

1942   General Manager/Dramatic Director Richard Kay requested a leave of absence to enter the armed services

1946   Full time Managing Director hired – Gordon Klein

1947   Took over store west of lobby for check room

The Lucier Theatre was purchased by LLT

Workshop and rehearsal hall building constructed

1948   Children's theatre reorganized under Dorothy Sanders and Jan Egert – Lakewood School of the Theater incorporated October 20, 1938, including instruction in theater, dance, drawing, painting, ceramics, and music therapy

Drama Production Wing organized

1949   The Women's Committee paid to have a pay phone installed in the lounge for the convenience of the patrons

1954   Artistic and managing director was hired – Karl Mackey

Started adult classes in speech and drama – Karl Mackey, instructor

1955   Held drama classes for college credit in cooperation with Fenn College

1958   LLT Fine Arts Foundation established

1959   Took over another store for Children's Theatre classroom

1963   LLT purchases a parcel east of the building for $100,000, which once held a laundromat, garage, and used car lot, as well as adjacent properties with single- and two-family dwellings

1965   Acquired new rehearsal hall and classroom building on parking lot property

LLT becomes a member of the Lakewood Chamber of Commerce

1967   Installed central air conditioning and heating

1969   Installed new carpeting and new seats; remodeled lobby, box office and ladies room

1972   Lakewood Mayor Robert Lawther introduces Ken Beck to Karl Mackey

1974   Ken Beck's fundraising challenge to the community; Architect Fred Toguchi began planning

Two parcels on Rockway Avenue under foreclosure were acquired

1975   Groundbreaking for The Kenneth C. Beck Center for the Cultural Arts/Lakewood Little Theatre

Cost of construction was estimated at $2,000,000, and LLT had raised $1,200,000. First Federal Savings and Loan Association organized an interbank agreement with three other Savings and Loans in Lakewood to provide a loan of $1 million to LLT to cover the project

1976   The Center opens on October 22 with Maxwell Anderson's *Mary, Queen of Scots* and classes begin

The organization's name officially changes to The Kenneth C. Beck Center for the Cultural Arts/Lakewood Little Theatre and address established as 17801 Detroit Avenue

Dance Education Department established

1977   Ken Beck dies in September

1983 The National Guard sells Armory on Wayne Avenue to the City of Lakewood which leases it to Beck Center

1984 The Lucier Theatre was split into three spaces: the lobby becomes a pottery studio, the theater is divided into the dance studio and the Studio Theater.

Studio Theater opens with *Lizzie Borden in the Late Afternoon*

1986 Karl Mackey retires after 32 years

1987 Organization name officially changes to "Beck Center for the Cultural Arts" on February 27, 1987

1991 The sale of the Armory from the City of Lakewood to Beck Center is complete

1992 Scott Spence becomes Artistic Director

1998 Cleveland Artists Foundation enters into 10-year lease in Beck Center main building

1999 Beginning of collaboration with Rock & Roll Hall of Fame, "Toddler Rock"

The theater program converted from "community theater" to "non-equity professional" status and actors are paid stipend wages.

2000 Riverside Academy of Music merges with Beck Center; the annex building at Rockway and Detroit Avenues is purchased.

Edward Gallagher becomes Director of Education

Extensive remodeling of Armory into classrooms

2002 Annual Razzle Dazzle production begins at Beck Center

Dance Alliance of Beck Center (DABC) is founded, Carol Culp as president

2004 Men's Advisory Board disbands due to dwindling number of members

2006 Beck Center's Board considers and rejects an idea to move the organization to Crocker Park in Westlake, Ohio

An economic impact study is commissioned by Impact Economics, an independent research firm, determining Beck Center has an economic impact of $10 million per year in Cuyahoga County

2007 Lucinda Einhouse becomes President & CEO

2010 Beck Center's CEO Cindy Einhouse becomes a member of the Commission on Economic Inclusion, committing to participate in an annual employer's survey on diversity and studying best practices in organizational leadership on diversity and inclusion

2011 The organization's name officially changes to "Beck Center for the Arts" on August 26, 2011

Beck Executive Committee meets to discuss the subject of diversity in the context of the Cleveland Foundation's "Engaging the Future" initiative. A takeaway from that meeting was that racial and ethnic diversity is important, as is diversity of sexual orientation

Beck Center receives The Commission 50 designation which recognized 50 organizations (25 for-profit, 25 non-profit/government) with the highest combined scores on Board, senior management, workforce and supplier diversity on the Commission's Employers Survey on Diversity

2012   Beginning of collaboration, co-productions with Baldwin Wallace University's Music Theatre program

TABC (Theater Alliance of Beck Center) is formed, Jeff Silver-Riskin as president. Previously the group was known as the Educational Theatre board and then C.A.S.T. (Company of Advocates for Students in Theater)

2014   Beck Center receives a letter from Governor of Ohio John Kasich extending congratulations and recognition of Beck Center as a leader in developing strong collaborative partnerships and promoting diversity in Northeast Ohio. He references Beck Center's annual collaboration with the Hispanic Cultural Center, Esperanza, and American Greetings celebrating National Hispanic Heritage Month

2016   *Creating Our Future* capital campaign begins

2019   Beck Center faculty and staff completes "Safe Zone" training, conducted by the LGBT Center of Cleveland, and develops an action plan

2020   Global pandemic begins – complete shutdown of all Ohio businesses on March 13

2021   Opening of the newly renovated Fowler-Spellman Education Wing; ribbon cutting on March 10, 2021

2022   Dedication of the newly renovated Center for Music and Creative Arts Therapies ("The M/CAT Building") on March 10, 2022

APPENDIX I - Directors in Lakewood Little Theatre & Beck Center History (Those who directed 10 or more productions) – as of January 2022

Compiled by John Jefferson

Karl Mackey	173
Scott Spence	114
Richard Kay	44
Gordon D. Klein	27
Sarah May	21
Fred Sternfeld	20
L. Bramer Carlson	18
William Roudebush	17
Charles Robinson	16
Paul Yaple	13
Hank Czekalinski	12
Victoria Bussert	12
James "Bud" Binns	10

APPENDIX J – Beck Center Board of Directors 2022

Patricia Oliver, Chair (Retired Partner, Tucker Ellis LLP)
Douglas Hoffman, Immediate Past Chair (Retired Architect, Weber Murphy Fox)
Lucinda Einhouse, President & CEO*
Cindy Brogan, Treasurer (Retired Vice President, Treasurer at The Sherwin-Williams Company)
Ellen Z. Todia, Secretary (Real Estate Developer)

Michael Brown (Former Managing Director in Loan Syndications, Huntington Bank)
Jane Christyson (Chief Executive Officer, Girl Scouts of North East Ohio)
Rosemary E. Corcoran (Retired, Development, Sisters of Charity Health System)
Syma Dar (Director of Adult Psychiatric Services at Fairview Hospital)
Michael Daso (Financial Consultant, Equitable Advisors)
Chann Fowler-Spellman (Co-Executive Director, The Char and Chuck Fowler Family Fdn)
Richard Fox (Retired, Vice President Corporate Controller, Sisters of Charity)
Frances Floriano Goins (Attorney, Ulmer & Berne LLP)
Emily Jett (Learning and Development, Protiviti)
Angie Kazi (Vice President, Relationship Manager, Bank of America Merrill Lynch)
Sean Malloy (Attorney, McDonald Hopkins)
Kathleen McGorray PhD (Education Consultant)
Ryan McKean (Financial Advisor, Turning Point Wealth)
Mickey Mencin (Retired Director of Corporate Marketing, Hyland Software)
Michael J. O'Brien (Retired Tax Partner, Deloitte Tax LLP)
Barbara Paynter (President, Paynter Communications LLC)
Amy Petrus (President, Petrus HR Solutions – Your Partner In HR)
Jeffery Poore (Procurement Manager – Northern Ohio, Turner Construction)
John A. Reynolds (Retired, Watson Wyatt & Co.)
Bradford Richmond, M.D. (Radiologist, Cleve Clinic)
Sandra Sauder (Community Leader)
Brian Sinchak (President, Lkwd Catholic Academy)
William Spence (Senior Human Resources Business Partner, KeyBank)
Corey Donovan Tracey (Principal, Jackson Lewis)
Thomas C. Wagner (Attorney, Thomas C. Wagner, LLC)
Margaret G. Weitzel (Retired Executive Vice President/Partner, Wyse Advertising)

Honorary – Ex Officio
Marianne Monahan, President, Women's Bd

Honorary
Ruth Bertrand
Nancy B. Calcott
Dr. David C. Estrop
Terry L. Jones
Andrew L. Killian
William J. Schmitt

National Board: Alice Ripley and Martin Savidge

CHAPTER 13:

Acknowledgements and Credits

Special thanks to:

- A special group of Beck lovers and history buffs who met many Friday mornings between April 2021 and January 2022 with Cindy Einhouse to rummage through the archives, edit drafts, and share ideas:
    - Rosemary Corcoran (Beck Board member since 1987 and past President of the Board)
    - Kathleen McGorray (Beck Board member since 2015 and Board Member of Lakewood Historical Society)
    - Lynda Sackett (see footnote # 3)
    - Sandra Sauder (Beck Board member since 2019 and Co-Chair of *Creating Our Future*)
- The dynamic Beck marketing staff of Julie Gilliland and Ryan Lucas for review, edit, and polish of this book
- Tim and Nancy Callahan for review and essential assistance with photo scanning
- Mike Linton for marketing expertise and support
- Rory O'Malley and Michael Chernus for providing photos and testimonials
- Jennifer Wynn for providing insight, detailed and valuable edits, and friendship
- Campaign Co-Chair and Past Board Chair Douglas Hoffman for review and edit, along with unstoppable dedication and encouragement through every endeavor
- Beck Board Chair Patricia Oliver for her brave, effective leadership through the pandemic and her incredible on-going support of the CEO in every way possible
- Lakewood Historical Society, Cleveland Institute of Art, Rock & Roll Hall of Fame, and The Plain Dealer for assistance with photos
- Steven Auvil (Squire Patton Boggs US LLP) for review and guidance
- Frank Dutton who provided research and articles about the Lucier Movie Theatre
- All the previous LLT/Beck staff members who wrote the (un-named author) histories and grant reports over the past decades, which provided much good information for this book
- Nick Brodella (since passed away) who conducted numerous interviews in 1994-1995 and worked hard on organizing the archives at that time
- Anna (Anastasia) Hertelendy – marketing intern summer of 2021 who worked on organizing Beck Center's massive archive collection
- John Jefferson for his input and edits, and for compiling a master list of all the actors, directors, and productions for the Beck archives (July – December 2021)
- Wally Senney, Bertram "Bud" Maheu, Jr. (Durham, NC), Carole Maheu Ritter (Easton, PA), and Maggie Maheu Milburn (Bay Village, OH) for providing family information
- Paul Kiser (married to Sara 'Saralinda' Seibert Kiser) who happened to contact Beck Center in September 2021, researching family history and the "Guild of the Masques," aka the "Lakewood Little Theatre," aka Beck Center for the Arts, as an important point in that history. Paul Kiser provided input about the Kay and Seibert families, as did Rebecca Seibert
- Don McBride, Rebecca Niemiec, Rennie Tisdale, Larry Goodpaster, Ed Gallagher, John Jefferson for reviewing drafts

Acknowledgements and Credits (continued)

Special thanks to:

- Georgia Burley, Shirley Lutts, and Cynthia Fisher who shared photos, notes, and files
- Michael Gill and Don McBride for input
- William Barrow, John Grabowski, Rick Sicha, Marcia Moll, Shawn Leininger, Peter Ketter, and Michael Fleenor for providing information and advice

(clockwise from the top) – Lynda Sackett, Sandra Sauder, Kathleen McGorray, Rosemary Corcoran, Cindy Einhouse

62666346R00109